THE ART OF PHOTOPLAY MAKING

BY

VICTOR OSCAR FREEBURG, Ph.D.

Author of "Disguise Plots in Elizabethan Drama"

"The alterations of scenes, so it be quietly and without noise, are things of great beauty and pleasure: for they feed and relieve the eye."

FRANCIS BACON

New York

THE MACMILLAN COMPANY

1918

THE ART OF
PHOTOPLAY MAKING

THE MACMILLAN COMPANY
NEW YORK · BOSTON · CHICAGO · DALLAS
ATLANTA · SAN FRANCISCO

MACMILLAN & CO., Limited
LONDON · BOMBAY · CALCUTTA
MELBOURNE

THE MACMILLAN CO. OF CANADA, Ltd.
TORONTO

THE VENUS OF MILO
See Index.

FOREWORD

You, O reader of the divine average, and I, often disgusted by the " movies," have sworn that we would never again go to see them. But, directly our solemn decision was made, we discovered that we could not keep our children or our grandparents away; so we had to break our vows and go again to see what our dear ones were seeing.

Now, since we cannot stop going to the motion picture theatres, let us find out as soon as possible which photoplays are ugly, and which are not so ugly; or, put it the other way, which are fair, and which are more beautiful. That means a little discussion. The " kiddies " and the old folks and you and I will all join in, and if we make the discussion loud enough and can decide what we really like and want, maybe the exhibitors, and the manufacturers, and the directors, and the scenario writers will pay attention.

In order to make my end of the discussion as loud as possible I have set it down in this book. Some of these ideas, I have, in fact, already expressed publicly in a series of lectures delivered at Columbia University between the autumn of 1915 and the spring of 1917, and in newspaper articles published during the same period in Sunday editions of *The New York Times, The New York Sun,* and *The Morning Telegraph.*

There are at least three other books which should be at hand and open. The first is Mr. Epes Winthrop

FOREWORD

Sargent's *Technique of the Photoplay,* which discusses the practical side of plot building, scenario writing, and photoplay filming; the second is the late Hugo Muensterberg's *The Photoplay,* which analyzes the laws of the human mind in connection with the motion picture; and the third is Mr. Vachel Lindsay's *Art of the Moving Picture,* which makes it perfectly clear that a motion picture, if properly thought out and manufactured, will contain the kind of beauty which we used to look for only in paintings and sculpture.

The producers have hired publicity men who publish little articles about the photoplays in the newspapers. These little articles are camouflaged so as to look like criticisms, but they deceive no one; even the tiny children know that they are really advertisements. They are no more true than the stupendous, stultifying statements on the bill posters of P. T. Barnum's three-ringed circus.

After all, just why should these publicity men tell us what they want us to want? Why shouldn't we ourselves tell them what we really want?

V. O. F.

U. S. Naval Training Camp
Pelham Bay Park
January 28, 1918

CONTENTS

ILLUSTRATIONS OF GOOD OR BAD PICTORIAL COMPOSITION

CONTENTS

ILLUSTRATIONS

THE ART OF
PHOTOPLAY MAKING

CHAPTER I

THE NEW ART

It is a common error to judge the photoplay by the standards of the stage drama, and to condemn it because it cannot do exactly what the stage drama can do. That the photoplay is silent and practically wordless is a fact, but this fact is really no more to be deplored than that sculpture is without colouring and that music is invisible. The man who deals with facts instead of prejudices must consider the limitations of the respective arts, not as defects, but as differentiating qualities.

When we examine the photoplay as an art medium we discover that it inherits something from each of the elder arts, and yet differs essentially from them all. Thus although a cinematic composition is a play of silent pictures and not of spoken words, it inherits from stage drama the power of delineating human characters in a series of actions interpreted by actors. It inherits from the art of acting and from stage pantomime some of the methods of this visual presentation; yet the photoplay, because of its ubiquity of setting and its hundreds of screen devices, has a flexibility which permits the representation of stories that no dramatist or director of stage pantomime would ever dream of undertaking.

It inherits something, too, from masques and pageants. Griffith's mobilization of large masses of people for dramatic effect on the screen may recall to some historian the visual appeal and dramatic power of a thousand trained mummers in a Roman triumph or a mediaeval masque. No doubt Griffith might have much to learn from these splendid forms of art if they could be conjured up for him to see. But the difference between crowds in a masque or in real life and crowds on the screen may be inferred from Griffith's own words, taken from an interview with him concerning his work at the western battle fronts. He said: "No single human being has ever actually seen a battle in the present war. . . . What the general sees, plus what his colonels see, and what his majors see, and the captains, lieutenants, sergeants, corporals and privates see, added up, would give a fair idea of what great modern battles look like. In other words, it takes 10,000 eyes to see such a battle, and no living creature has that many eyes. Only the motion picture camera has 10,000 eyes."

The photoplay inherits much from the art of painting. The essential feature of the motion picture is, of course, that it actually records and transmits visible motion. And the photoplay as such is a single composition of these pictorial motions. The cinema composer is the artist who conceives these motions originally, relates them mentally to each other in some definite unity, prescribes and directs their production, and finally unites the cinematographed records into a film, and if the principles of pictorial composition have been applied in the making, this film will reveal pictorial beauty when projected on the screen.

To this statement some painter may reply, " Nonsense; we painters have the monopoly of pictorial beauty." Let him say what he pleases, so long as he does not hide his paintings under a bushel, because from those paintings, or from the masterpieces of centuries gone by, the cinema composer may learn the principles of pictorial composition. And, even though these principles may not be altered by a new use, they will in the hands of the cinema composer produce pictorial beauty of a new type.

Even sculpture may be searched for its secret of appeal, and the secret told to the makers of photoplays. Is not sculpture impressive mainly for the reason that the appreciator inspects it from many angles and many distances until clearness and emphasis result from the repetition of effects or meanings? Repetition is also the fundamental means of emphasis in music. And as music is a movement of ever arising, ever vanishing sounds, with certain recurring motifs, so a cinematic composition may effectively be a movement of ever arising, ever vanishing visual values, with certain recurring pictorial motifs.

The photoplay further inherits or adapts the methods of the novelist. It is the novelist's privilege to follow his characters wherever they go, no matter how often the scene may shift. This, too, is the privilege of the cinema composer. The camera may follow the hero indoors and out, into lonely places or crowded streets, into peaceful privacy or public broil, until the audience, virtually behind the camera, are made intimately acquainted with him and become eagerly interested in his career.

The novelist resorts to words, and the stage director resorts to paint and canvas, in order to reproduce the various settings which constitute the hero's environment. But the cinema composer may go directly to the natural setting and bring it back to his audience, mysteriously real, yet operative as an element in art. And, for the first time in the history of narrative representation, nature herself may be made to play an important rôle. Real settings may further be manipulated in the photoplay so that architecture and landscape gardening are brought to join their artistic effect with the main pictorial and dramatic impression of the play.

Hence, a photoplay is not to be considered a novel in celluloid. A recent review in the New York *Herald* contains the statement: "*Les Misérables,* a motion picture drama adapted from the epic novel of Victor Hugo, was presented at the Lyric Theatre after several months of preparation. The photoplay probably is as close an approach to literature as has been accomplished on the screen." Does this reviewer look upon a photoplay as art or as commercial imitation? If he were commenting on a piece of sculpture would he praise it because it was probably as close an approach to painting as had been accomplished in marble?

Besides the more or less obvious inheritances from the elder arts the motion picture play has, of course, its own unique powers, powers that are newly discovered and still being tested. The mysterious appeal of visible motion in nature is now for the first time being adapted to the uses of art. The supernatural, which has been written about in poetry and fiction, and talked about in plays, is now for the first time exhibited before our eyes through the magic of the cinematograph.

Thus we shall see that a photoplay is a very complicated thing, involving many elements of expression and many principles of composition. To select and control all these elements, to learn and apply all these principles, requires a mind of extraordinary patience, alertness, and ingenuity. But if the numerous parts that go into a photoplay can be welded by the fire of genius into a harmonious whole, the result may be a piece of art. It may contain entertainment, or beauty, or truth, or inspiration, or all of these, for the audience, and it may in its peculiar composition reveal the taste and temperament of its composer.

Now if this piece of art is neither literature, nor stage drama, nor painting, nor sculpture, nor music, nor architecture, but something else, distinct from these arts, though affiliated with them, it must be judged and appraised as a new art. But there can be no fair appraisement without knowledge. There can be no helpful criticism of a new art without sympathetic insight into its special scope and its unique possibilities. What the photoplay world needs at present is more definite canons of criticism. It needs critics of taste and training expressing themselves in the periodicals and newspapers; it needs careful studies in book form; it needs photoplay leagues; it needs to be protected against the inartistic no less than against the immoral; it needs most of all something which will in time result from the constructive criticism of specialists, a general knowledge and understanding on the part of the public of just what it is they would rather see on the screen than the inanity and hodgepodge that now so often claim their attention.   There is no doubt that the public can be trusted to form good taste providing it is given something good to taste.   In the future it may be that any given photoplay will be re-filmed over and over again until something like perfection results.   It may be, too, that the motion picture machine will take its place in our homes along with the phonograph; but this will not come until films become worthy of repeated exhibition as favorite art treasures.

The photoplay as art is twenty-five hundred years younger than the stage play.   It is still in its infancy; and infancy is the age of experimentation.   Whether this experimentation shall be intelligently directed toward the end of mature potentiality depends on the united efforts of authors, critics, and casual appreciators.

CHAPTER II

THE PSYCHOLOGY OF THE CINEMA AUDIENCE

THE manufacturer of photoplays studies his audience through the box office. To him there are two kinds of audiences, the good and the small. He calls a given photoplay ninety-five percent perfect if ninety-five out of a hundred local exhibitors report good audiences on the particular day or week when the play was exhibited. But we as students or critics or serious minded photoplaywrights cannot afford to make hasty inferences from the mere facts of dollars and houses. If we are to improve the photoplay as art we need to penetrate more philosophically into the nature of the audience, we need to understand the experience of the average member of that audience, his reactions, sensations, feelings, and thoughts during the exhibition of a picture. As practical artists we must see our goal before we start, we must address our message before we send it. And we should know our audience before we attempt to communicate with it.

It must never be forgotten that the theatre audience is a crowd. A crowd is a compact mass of people held together by a single purpose during any period of time whether long or short. The various units are in close contact with each other, the crowd existing as such only while this close contact is maintained. In the theatre a particular crowd exists as such only during the time of the performance and can never exist again once it has been broken up after the particular performance for which it came together.   The close contact is spiritual as well as physical.   You not only touch elbows with your neighbour and live in his atmosphere but you are infected by his emotions and share his desires, purposes, reactions.   This close contact gives the crowd a peculiar psychology.   The individual in the crowd is not the same as when alone.   He is subconsciously influenced by his companions or neighbours until his emotions are heightened and his desire or ability to think is lowered.   He laughs more easily and at less comic things in a crowd than when he is alone.   In the crowd he is more responsive, more demonstrative, more kind, more cruel, more sentimental, more religious, more patriotic, more unreasoning, more gullible than when alone.   A crowd, therefore, is more emotional and less intellectual than its members were before they came together.

While the crowd is single-minded the public is many-minded.   The public may be looked upon as a vast web-like association of unified groups, families, cliques, coteries, leagues, clubs, and crowds.   A crowd can never exist as such for more than three or four hours at a time, or while the close contact is maintained and the single interest is held.   But a public may have space between its units and time between its sessions.   Furthermore, the public is permanent in its existence.   Its groups come in contact, though not simultaneously; views are exchanged, discussions are carried on, letters are written, until as a result of all this reflection a deliberate expression is arrived at.   This deliberate expression is called public opinion.

But a crowd by its very nature never has time to re-flect. It must decide and act on instinct or impulse or, at best, on the first flash of thought. After that crowd has been broken up, the individuals may upon reflection reverse their decisions. These second thoughts, these mature judgments may then become a part of public opinion. It happens, therefore, very often that political orators — we need mention no names — can sway crowds but cannot sway the public. It happens too that a play may be applauded by three or fifteen or fifty crowds and yet not finally make for itself a public. This is so because the crowd grasps at the obvious and immediate, because it is impressed by surface values. But a play cannot become a permanent possession of civilization unless its values are deep, fundamental, vital, subtle, and permanent; unless, in short, it will stand the test of study and time.

Classic stage plays such as *Macbeth* or *The School for Scandal* or *Lady Windermere's Fan* have stood this test and have their public, who will attend a performance whether done by college dramatic society, society amateurs, or the best professional talent. And, through their masterpieces, dramatists like Shakespeare, Sheridan, Wilde, Shaw, Maeterlinck, and Barrie have their public, who will be interested in any play, no matter how obscure or inferior, attributed to these authors. But in the brief history of the photoplay no scenario writer has succeeded in winning a public. It is true that Mr. Griffith has a public; but he is a director and producer as well as a writer. At present not one photoplay out of a hundred gets a public. The momentary nature of exhibition prevents it. Photoplays are seen and judged by single isolated crowds, in Boston and Kalamazoo and Galveston, but rarely by a steady succession of crowds in one place, a succession that might finally develop a public criticism. There are exceptions, of course, such as *Cabiria, The Birth of a Nation,* and *Intolerance.*

But in the motion picture world it is the " star," the actor or actress, who gets the public. Mary Pickford has her public. Francis Bushman has his. The Drews and Chaplin have theirs. Here again the conditions of exhibition are responsible. A play is flashed upon the screen, fades away, and dies with that performance. It lives again somewhere, perhaps in Brooklyn or Hoboken, but not for us. We cannot read it. Nor can we find it or see it again at will. It exists only for a crowd. The plays go; but the " stars " remain. In the same theatre we may applaud them again tomorrow or next week. They will exhibit their powers in a new story, a new " vehicle," but we give the " vehicle " casual attention, because we know that it, too, will be whisked away. Meanwhile we become familiar with the performers. We know their names, and ages, and favourite amusements. We criticize them. We tell our friends that they are not so wonderful as advertised to be, or that every one must be sure to see them. Thus under present conditions the interpreter, rather than the play, secures a firm grasp upon the public.

Yet these difficult conditions in the motion picture world need not discourage the cinema composer. If he can only capture enough crowds, say a thousand or more, he, too, will ultimately win a public, providing, of course, that the surface appeal which pleased the crowd will, when penetrated, reveal a deeper appeal capable of holding the public.   But how can he coax even one crowd into captivity?   If the cinema composer studies the psychology of the spectators in a motion picture theatre he will discover that for them three classes of appeal exist in every film that tells a story.   They are: first, the sense appeal to the eye; second, the emotional appeal; and, third, the intellectual appeal.   The sense appeal and emotional appeal are primary, elemental, and strong, while the intellectual appeal is secondary and relatively slight.

The visual sense of the spectator reacts first to the beauty of the subject photographed.   Thus a moonlit lake, a surf-swept beach, spruce-covered foothills, an Italian villa near a mountain pass, the interior of a richly furnished mansion — all give the eye a sensation of pleasure, a pleasure which is quite apart from their meaning, their relation to the plot of the play. The spectator might be too stupid to understand the story and yet might thoroughly enjoy the picture. This delight of the eye is a primitive sensation; yet it is experienced by every spectator whether he be an infant or a mature man of culture.   It is more than an appreciation of a picture; it is a delight in the subject itself.   The spectator easily imagines that he is in direct contact with the beautiful reality itself, and forgets that the camera has intervened.

The eye is especially pleased by certain types of physical movement which the motion picture can transmit, and which cannot be transmitted through any other art medium.   When a pebble is thrown into a pool a number of circular ripples immediately take form and, expanding in concentric rings, finally flatten out and lose themselves in the still surface of the pool. The eye is pleased by these expanding ripples and by the endless multiplication of rings which rise mysteriously from the point where the pebble went down. The eye does not discover any particular meaning in this subject; it merely enjoys the abstract motion. If motion were absent, and the rings were still, as they would seem in an ordinary photograph, there would be no sense of visual pleasure. Other examples of pure motion pleasing to the eye are the pouring rush of a waterfall, the rhythmic undulations of the sea, the fan-like spreading of a sky rocket, the slow curling of smoke from a factory funnel, the varying balance of a bird in flight, the steady forward thrust of a yacht under full sail. In all these subjects it is the continuous movement rather than the static moment which pleases the eye. And the motion picture is the new and unique medium through which these movements may be reproduced with artistic effect.

There is a keen pleasure of the eye also when appealing motion identifies itself with the expression of the human body, individually as in the case of a dancer, and *en masse* as in the case of a regiment on parade. This response of our senses to human form and physical movement is primary and elemental, and takes place before our brain has time to interpret the dramatic significance of the visible stimulus. Hence we see that a fundamental duty of the photoplaywright is to give the performers full scope for the physical appeal, and to set their action amid an environment which shall instantly impress the eye of the spectator. This first impression on the observer is tremendously important. And the scenario writer must remember that it is his business to furnish good subjects for the director, and that both he and the director must conspire with the photographer to captivate the eye of the audience, because whatever other appeals a photoplay is to make, it must first appeal to the eye.

While the spectator at a photoplay feels the visual or purely physical sensation described above, his spiritual experience is enriched by the emotions which are being kindled by the play. We have already said that the crowd is very highly susceptible to emotional appeal, that the individual in the crowd is more emotional than when alone. His emotional experience is of a twofold nature. He feels what we may call " self-emotion," or emotion which has no reference to any person in the play or to any other person in the world, and he feels a social emotion, a feeling of social relation with, and a personal interest in, the characters of the play. The self-emotion in the cinema theatre when viewing a pictured scene, is like the self-emotion in real life face to face with real nature. We have all experienced it, yet cannot easily describe it. Sometimes it may be a vague sense of longing as we look through the slender birches across a wide bay at the low majesty of the spruce-covered bank beyond. But the longing does not formulate itself. We do not know exactly what we want or feel. It is a mysterious mingling of contentment and sadness. In the same way the eternal whiteness of an Alpine peak, a dim sail on the far horizon, the luminous reflection of a summer cloud in a mountain lake — all stir in us an emotion of silent marvel or wonder or a vague longing for something — something beyond our present experience. Sometimes the self-emotion may be more naïve, a thrill or excitement at some action or disturbance, at a street crowd rushing to a fight or a fire, even when we are not quite sure or do not really care what it is all about. The sense of an incipient or impending stir outside us stimulates a corresponding agitation within us, and we are impressed before we really know what it is that has impressed us. The spectator in the motion picture theatre easily yields to these simple emotional appeals. He surrenders to the illusion of art, and easily imagines that he is in the presence of real nature or of the actual original action.

But the spectator's emotional experience is still more vivid in his dramatic sympathy, his social interest in the characters on the screen. The fact that social emotions can be aroused by something which is confessedly not real, by mere pictures of people who do not exist except in imagination, is of fundamental importance in dramatic or literary art. This illusion makes drama a tremendous power. It makes our world very large and our human acquaintance very wide. Fiction becomes real. Fictitious characters become more real even than their authors. To us Shylock seems more real than Shakespeare. We could almost believe that the Jew was a historical figure and the Englishman only a myth. Don Quixote, Sherlock Holmes, and Peter Pan surely are more real than Cervantes, Conan Doyle, and Barrie. We know the characters of story so intimately because through the medium of art we have come in personal contact with them, have admired their powers, or sympathized with their joys and sorrows. In the motion picture theatre this illusion of personal contact with the characters is especially strong. We admire or dislike, love or hate, approve or disapprove, forgive or refuse to forgive, these mere shadows on the screen. We select our friends from among the heroes and heroines, but we scorn the villainous, the stupid, and the low. We weep real tears over sorrows which we know do not really exist. We applaud triumphs which we know are never really achieved. We have definite fears and dreads and hopes and ambitions for merely imaginary characters.

These social emotions arise in us, not only because we are sympathetically interested in the outcome of any human struggle, as we shall see in a later chapter, but because, by a law of psychology, we project our very selves into the characters on the screen. Thus every spectator in the audience may get by proxy the experiences and emotions of the character he is observing. The identification of self with fictitious characters is especially true of childhood. Lovers of Dickens will remember David Copperfield's statement that as a child his only and constant comfort was reading novels, putting himself into all the good characters and putting Mr. Murdstone, his hated stepfather, and Miss Murdstone into all the bad ones. In the theatre today the little girl identifies herself with the queen or with the adventuress. She imagines herself as magnificent as one and as clever as the other. The little boy identifies himself vividly with the hero in all his nobility or with the villain in all his shrewdness. It is human nature to crave an increasing experience, an experience which is not limited by the boundaries of circumstance, or propriety. Where actuality imprisons us, art sets us free. In art the janitor may become a king, the postman, a general; you may become a train robber, your sister, a vampire, and I may become a millionaire. Thus all of us may get vicariously the experience which we could not get or would not want in actual life.

An interesting representation of this projecting of self into a character may be found in the Blue Bird photoplay *Undine*. The film represents a man reading the story of *Undine* to his little girl. When they get to the part about the fisherman's child the little girl says to her father, " I want to be their little girl." The father gives her permission, and through the rest of the film we see the rôle of the fisherman's child played by the same girl who sat on her father's knee and listened to the reading of the story about that child.

One of the factors involved in our sympathies with the characters on the stage or on the screen is the factor of the performer who plays the part. After having seen Sarah Bernhardt in *Camille* or David Warfield in *The Music Master* or John Barrymore in *Justice* we can never think of the chief characters in those plays respectively except in connection with the performers. A reading of the play in book form before or after it is acted does not make the stamp of the actor's personality any less indelible. In the case of the photoplay where the film version is the only one, the coalescence of the actor with the part he plays is even more complete. In fact it would be impossible for us to come in contact with the photoplay character at all except through the photographed pantomime of the performer. Therefore in the photoplay our social emotions toward the characters are largely conditioned by our like or dislike of the actor or actress.

In fact, the " movie fan " is quite content to admire acting apart from its significance in the interpretation of character. His eagerly surrendered dime is a tribute to the physical skill or daring of a fellow being, some comedian who rolls humorously down a flight of stairs, or some actress who leaps from a racing automobile to the cow-catcher of a train. This is an elemental and primitive emotion. For thousands of years gaping humanity has been thrilled by the juggler and the acrobat. And who of us has not inherited this savage appreciation? Which of us does not some time steal away from the press of business, the depths of philosophy, or the heights of art to thrill at the gifts of the baseball pitcher, the prize fighter, or the cabaret dancer? Such admiration of physical skill in a fellow being is basic in all the appreciation we have for theatrical performance. Julia Marlowe and Charlie Chaplin, antipodal as they may seem, have built their success on the same foundation, this social emotion of the crowd, this admiration of physical ability in a fellow. The crowd by no means objects to well-developed characters in a play, but it demands that these characters shall be conceived or adjusted to reveal the powers of favourite actors or actresses. Any theatre crowd, except one composed of dramatists and critics, would rather see a first class actor in a second class play than a second class actor in a first class play. This emphasizes what we have already said, that the crowd grasps at the obvious and immediate, and is impressed by surface values. The actor is the surface value of the character he interprets. In the case of the good actor this surface value is an accurate index to the character which lies beneath.

In the case of the bad actor the surface value is like a gaudy curtain which prevents our seeing the character created by the author. In either case the eye of the crowd feeds eagerly upon the show of the surface.

Here then is the moral. If the cinema composer wishes to arouse the social emotions of the crowd, if he wishes to give every spectator a personal escape into the fascinating region of vicarious experience, he must conceive and delineate his characters in the terms of the greatest acting values. The emotions of an audience are the treasure trove of the artist; and for the time being the motion picture " star " is the only one who can unlock it.

The intellectual appeal of a photoplay is slight compared with its emotional appeal. The momentary, flashing nature of exhibition and the psychology of the crowd give the spectator little opportunity or desire to exercise his intellectual faculties. Yet he has certain intellectual experiences while seeing a photoplay. The fundamental one is the satisfaction of curiosity. We constantly desire new material to add to our store of knowledge. We crave novelty. The average American scans his newspaper with bated breath. But the recognition of a thing as new is an intellectual process. Our judgment declares a thing new by comparing it with the old which we already possess. Then the new itself becomes old and the adventure of the mind must begin again. Only yesterday the motion picture itself was a kind of novelty. With rapt attention we observed: " The picture moves! " " It doesn't hurt our eyes! " " Things look so real! " " How clever the photographer is! "

Today the mechanical devices of story telling on the screen are still new. The devices of leaders, cut-ins, close-ups, flash-backs, visions, dissolving views, fade-outs, fade-ins, double exposures, dual rôles, etc., have a strong appeal of novelty. In the light of his experience the spectator recognizes these processes as new; and he is eager to see the next play released because it may contain some new evidence of the mechanician's ingenuity.

Novelty of physical content appeals to the spectator as well as novelty of physical form. He eagerly satisfies his curiosity with regard to other places and climes, other people and phases of life than those with which he is familiar. The South Dakota cowboy finds novelty in the story which is laid in a Cape Cod fishing village or on board a millionaire's yacht. The child of the Ghetto finds the same novelty. The fisherman, the colonial dame, and the heiress find novelty in the bitter story of the Ghetto, or in the spacious drama of the South Dakota ranches. It matters little that these scenes may be " faked " by the producer of the film. The satisfaction of curiosity still takes place in the mind of the spectator. In fact, the illusion of the screen is so great that for the time the spectator feels that he is in direct contact with the reality. The impression will remain; and in the confused memory of old age this same spectator, though he has never traveled, will say, " When I was in Yokohama —" or " When I stood before the sphinx —" only to be interrupted by some indulgent grandchild who will explain, " You know, granddaddy was never there at all; he only saw those things in the ' movies '! "

Curiosity concerning surface structure of a play

and its physical content can always be successfully appealed to by the photoplaywright. But he will never find the crowd very much interested in the abstract principles and laws upon which a play is built. It has. no critical appreciation of craftsmanship. The trained cinema composer may show commanding ability in his mobilization of human materials for the play; he may show keen logic in the motivation of his action; he may show economic originality in dramatizing his pictorial setting; he may show great deftness in his plot weaving, and the crowd will sit through it all without a single æsthetic thrill. Æsthetic appreciation of workmanship is the result not of impulse but of analysis; and the play must become established as a public favourite before these values are discovered and admired. After a play has reached the public its chances of becoming a classic are multiplied by good craftsmanship; but good craftsmanship as such is of little value in helping the play to reach the public. Therefore it would be stupid for a photoplaywright to say, "It's strange this play didn't win the crowd; I'm sure it's perfectly constructed." In other words, craftsmanship is a means and not an end, as far as the audience is concerned. The author must design and contrive deftly, almost secretly, to please the senses and capture the emotions and add to the intellectual possession of the audience. The results are paramount, while the ingenuity and artistry of the methods will either be ignored or unrecognized. But, to return to our theme, the primary intellectual experience of the spectator during a photoplay is the satisfaction of curiosity, curiosity as to content, and curiosity as to the photographic devices of telling the story.

Another intellectual process is the recognition of comic value. We are amused when we are surprised into observing an incongruity, an example of human unfitness; we laugh because we know better. In a flash we compare the unfitness of the thing with what we know should be its fitness. This comparison is a momentary, subconscious intellectual process. To be sure, the tax on our subconscious judgment is very slight. It is almost absent in our appreciation of slapstick buffoonery. It is greatest in our appreciation of comedy of subtle or whimsical situation. In making comparisons between fitness and unfitness we naturally choose ourselves as examples of the former and the dramatic victims as examples of the latter. Thus we are more dignified than the clown who makes grimaces; we are more comfortable than the teacher who sits down upon a tack; we are more self-controlled than the talkative drunkard; we are wiser than the idiot who fears a stuffed bear; we are more sophisticated than the country lout who tries to mail letters in the fire alarm box. This sudden recognition of personal superiority pleases us to the point of laughter. A sensation of pleasure and a feeling of hilarity sets in, which sweep the cobwebs of care from our brains. The slight, almost neglible, mental effort of recognizing incongruity relieves the brain of all mental strain, the seriousness of real life is forgotten, and we abandon ourselves to the caprice of the sportive unreality on the screen.

It must be remembered that the motion picture makes

its appeal primarily through the eye. Hence it is only natural that the individual of the crowd, with his lowered intellectuality, should respond more easily to caricature of physical appearance and action than to the humour of situation which must be inferred from grasping the dramatic significance of the characters and their activities in the plot. In a following chapter we shall take up a more careful discussion of comedy in general and the possibilities of screen comedy in particular. Suffice it to say here that audiences are fond of comedy, and that they respond primarily to the kind of comedy which can be grasped visually, instantaneously, and with the least mental effort.

The process of comparison and judgment which we have just said is present in comic appeal, is a subconscious process of the mind. The opportunity of deliberately judging and reasoning would not be welcomed by the audience. The theatre crowd is neither willing nor fitted to weigh evidence and come to conclusions concerning questions of debate. The crowd is sentimental rather than philosophic. The crowd wants to see the lovers reunited at the end of the play; but it does not care to apportion the rewards of these characters according to the principles of absolute equity and justice. The crowd thrills at the proposition that no man shall treat his wife as though she were a mere chattel; but it would not warm up to a screen discussion of property rights. The crowd cheers the Stars and Stripes or a picture of the President; but it remains cold towards the tariff. The explanation of all this is that law, social science, and statesmanship require close application of thought and are only mildly diverting: and the audience wants the maximum of entertainment with the minimum of thinking. Mental receptivity is determined by mood; and the mood for visual pleasure and emotional thrill is not the mood for argument. The scenario writer must not infer from our discussion that his play may safely be brainless, but, on the other hand, he must not hope to impress the theatre crowd by the originality of his thinking, nor must he look to the photoplay as an easy medium for argumentative expression. It is true that, if he expects to reach the public and to hold it permanently, he must make the underlying philosophy of his composition sound and valid, but he must also see to it that this philosophy is underlying and not outstanding; because he cannot feed the crowd with philosophy unless he incases it in the sugar coating of emotional entertainment.

The most intense intellectual experience of the spectator during the exhibition of a photoplay is the state of suspense concerning the outcome of any given situation or of the plot as a whole. Mental suspense is the fundamental element of dramatic appeal, and no play could hold the interest of an audience without it. How to arouse and maintain suspense is so important a question that we shall devote a separate chapter to its discussion. Let us merely say here that suspense is a combination of emotional and intellectual experience. The spectator is in a state of thrill and wonder regarding the progress of action; at the same time he matches his wits with the author, playing the rôle of detective and prophet, and tries to forecast and anticipate the action. He observes alertly every detail of the plot and makes rapid inferences concerning the content of the pictures yet to be flashed on the screen. His attention is firmly fixed until the end of the action comes, when a mental relaxation sets in, which is as pleasant as rest after bodily exertion. Without suspense a photoplay is merely a succession of pictures, and can no more hold the unwavering attention of the spectator than a row of pictures on a museum wall. Such a play displeases the individual of the audience because it deprives him of the intense mental joy of being kept in a state of doubt, anxiety, and expectation concerning the progress and outcome of a dramatic action.

Suspense is a quick, cold process of the mind, but it is also a warm state of the heart; if it were not, the crowd, being highly emotional, would never desire it. Suspense, as we have said above, is dependent on social emotions, on a definite personal sympathy with the characters in the play, and a warm interest in their careers and fates.

The individual in the crowd is willing to think providing he may think with his heart. He is also willing to think providing he may think as he pleases. There is no intellectual activity easier and more restful than the play of fancy. It is easy because it is not constrained by law; the individual may let his mind rove where it pleases. It is restful because it gives him a refreshing escape from the hard, prosaic facts of everyday life. Since the spectator enjoys the exercise of his imagination the cinema composer should spare no effort to provide him with an opportunity for this mental exercise. The fascinating thing about the motion picture is that, although to a certain extent it robs the imagination by presenting photographically to the body's eye things which had hitherto been seen only by the mind's eye, yet it admits of many entirely new means and methods of appealing to the imagination. It will be interesting to analyze and illustrate in following chapters the possibilities of appealing to the spectator's sense of wonder as well as to his imagination in new ways through the medium of the motion picture.

Thus we have studied and tried to understand the nature and mood, the affections and aversions, the whims and reliabilities, the emotional impressionability and intellectual receptivity of the average crowd in the motion picture theatres. After the cinema composer has some notion of the psychology of the crowd, after he knows pretty clearly what his aim is to be, he may more intelligently decide upon his methods for accomplishing that aim. We are now facing our problem; let us try to discover the best methods of solving it. Let us learn how best to please the eye, how to stir the self-emotion of the individual in the crowd, how to arouse and maintain his social sympathies, how to give him intellectual entertainment without mental fatigue; and let us constantly remember that if our photoplay is to become a classic it must possess beneath the attractive surface which appeals to the crowd the permanent values of illuminating truth, universal meaning, and unfading beauty.

CHAPTER III

THE appeal of the photoplay is pictorial, as well as dramatic. It is an appeal directly to the eye, as well as to the heart and to the brain. But the dramatic appeal of the photoplay, that is, the appeal to the heart and the brain, is also through the pictorial. Therefore the main problem of the photoplay maker is to appeal simultaneously to the eye and through the eye. He must learn the art of producing pictures that are in themselves beautiful as pictures and at the same time in themselves significant and impressive as elements of a drama. Both of these laws must be obeyed if the product is to be called art. We have all seen dozens of photoplays which, though strong in plot, left us unsatisfied because they were pictorially displeasing, or not pleasing. And we have all seen photoplays which, though pictorially beautiful, failed to impress us because they were dramatically meaningless or weak. We realize, therefore, that here, as in any other art, the appreciator demands adequate and beautiful treatment as much as adequate and beautiful content. In the novel or the stage play the treatment is literary and the writer must attend carefully to his words and sentences. In the photoplay the treatment is pictorial and the cinema composer must attend carefully to his pictures and picture sequences, his pictorial moments and movements.

26

First of all a picture must be beautiful. It can neither please us nor impress us pictorially unless it is beautiful. A graphic representation which is ugly, or neither ugly nor beautiful, is not a picture. It has no pictorial appeal. It is merely an illustration or a practical record. I pick up a sales catalogue of Sears, Roebuck and Company, of Chicago, and as I glance through the pages I see the following illustrations: a sewing machine, a bed spring, an alarm clock, a monkey wrench, a woman stripped to a conspicuous corset. These representations are not beautiful pictorially because the subjects are not in themselves beautiful. I turn to an old kodak album and see a photograph of a young woman and a young man in a canoe. The exposure was made at a moment when a motor boat had just backed into the field of vision, and a United States flag at its stern almost completely conceals the face and figure of the young woman. And the camera was so tilted that the canoe seems to be sliding backward down hill. This photograph is not beautiful pictorially because the composition is bad; that is, because the subject matter, though sufficiently beautiful in itself, is badly treated. The examples given illustrate the two phases of pictorial ugliness, namely, ugliness of subject and ugliness of composition.

But what is beauty? Upon what grounds do we decide that a subject or an arrangement is beautiful? A completely analytic answer to these questions cannot be given here, but we should like to refer the reader to all the standard books on æsthetics that he can find. A recent little book by Violet Paget (" Vernon Lee ") entitled *The Beautiful* is especially to be recommended.   Miss Paget defines "the beautiful as implying an attitude of contemplative satisfaction." In another form her definition is, "Beautiful means satisfactory for contemplative, *i.e. for reiterated perception.*"   In other words, if you have a sense of satisfaction when you look upon a picture, and if the satisfaction remains when you look upon it long or again, or dwell upon it in memory, then that picture to you is beautiful.   Let us adopt that definition and proceed on the understanding that a cinema picture is beautiful when subject and composition together put the spectator in a state of contemplative satisfaction.

At this point some scenario writer may say, "Why should I worry about all this?   It is the business of the photographer and the director to produce pictures. I only produce plot."   To him we must reply, If you are a cinema composer at all, if you are endeavouring to compose a play in pictures instead of in words, then you must conceive, see clearly, and enable the director, actors, and photographer to actualize adequately the pictures, that is, the materials, which constitute your play.   A cinema composer who is not interested in seeing and shaping his own pictures would be like a singer who did not care to imagine his notes before singing them, or a poet who did not care to think his words before writing them.   Words must be thought before they can be written, notes must be heard, at least heard in imagination, before they can be sung, and cinema pictures must be seen in imagination before they can ever be seen in reality.   If the cinema composer hopes to achieve art he must become the master of his medium.   Furthermore, he must become the master of his servants, his workmen.   He must command, advise, and supervise the director, the actors, the photographer, the joiner, these workmen who are endeavouring to put into physical form the picture-play which he, the cinema composer, has conceived and developed in imagination.   It is true that under the present methods of production it seems commercially desirable to misinterpret, distort, vulgarize, or stultify the work of the author before it reaches the author's audience, but it is more true that if we all strive together we will some day bring about the state of affairs where the author is the master of all the forces which he mobilizes in expressing himself to an audience.

The scenario writer must not only imagine his pictures, but he must learn to imagine them in terms of the screen.   The following passage, taken from a scenario, is a clear evidence that the person who wrote it was not thinking in terms of the screen.   " ' I love her,' he soliloquizes as he sits in the moonlight on the broad piazza of his great home.   Suddenly a low voice in song comes to him, with the fragrance of dew-laden flowers, from the garden, like a nightingale."   The cinema composer must think of visibilities, not of fragrances or bird notes.   But even visibilities are not the same on the screen as in reality.   He must learn, for example, that on the screen a green meadow has the same tone and texture as a grey coat, that a red apple has the same tone and texture as a polished black shoe, that on the screen golden hair looks white, and red lips, black.   He must learn, for example, that a rapid movement squarely across the field of vision near the camera will photograph as a series of jerks,

this is not so.   A few tests will soon reveal to any one the fact that in many real or cinematographed actions it is a moment, rather than a movement, which impresses the eye and remains in the memory; that is, that in such actions the mind always retains a static instant, or tableau, rather than the movements which lead up to, or away from, that tableau.   Take the simple case of a man running.   The part of the step which we see most vividly and recall most easily is the moment when his legs are farthest apart, one forward and one backward.   This is true no matter from what angle we observe the runner.   When an instantaneous photograph is made of the runner it often happens that an unfamiliar moment is recorded by the camera, and we express surprise that a man could ever get his legs twisted into such a strange position.   The testimony of the photograph is proof that in the case of the runner our eyes grasp and our minds retain certain selected moments rather than the transitions, which consist of all of the moments in consecutive order.   Take the case of the stage drama.   Do you not remember certain instants, certain tableaux, more vividly than the transitions or movements between these tableaux?   It is beside the point to reply that your most vivid recollection is the sound of a voice or a word.   We are talking now of pictorial impressions.   Try to recall the pictorial aspects of the action in a play you saw years ago.   What do you recall?   Moments or movements?   Rarely a movement, more often a moment. The psychology of this emphasis is usually simple enough.   There was a momentary pause of the object or of some part of the object just after completing, or just before beginning, a movement.   This is true in the case of the runner's knee or foot. And this is true in the stage play, where the momentary pause is often deliberately produced and prolonged by the director in order to give the audience what he calls a " picture." The essential point to remember is that the " picture " or static moment is there whether the director tries to produce it or not.

A further explanation of our tendency to emphasize a pictorial moment is undoubtedly that our eyes and brains have been trained, from looking at paintings and sculpture, or at graphic representations of painting and sculpture, to expect and observe the pictorial pose and attitude of the subject in action. The painter or sculptor may suggest action, but he can never represent it. He can never represent more than a single instant of that action, but he knows from thousand year old traditions in art and from his own observation of æsthetic appeal to the eye what particular moment to seize upon, to arrest, and to fix in the permanence which endures longer than canvas or stone. We are all familiar with " The Discus Thrower " of Myron, a sculptor who lived four hundred and fifty years before Christ.[1] The athlete is represented at the moment when his arm is swung farthest back, and the discus is about to be hurled forward with full force. At the college track meet of today we observe and appraise the athlete's " form " at this same moment of his performance. The instantaneous composition of the college man's body may not be as pleasing to the eye as the composition of the sculptor's masterpiece, but whether pleasing or not the pictorial moment is there just the same.

[1] See page 30.

APOLLO AND THE MUSES

See Index.

The famous painting of " Apollo and the Muses " by Giulio Romano is an example of a pictorial moment during the action of a group of figures.[1]   Apollo and the nine muses are dancing in a circle.   If we examine the figures separately we see that each dancer is represented during the instantaneous pause between the completion of one movement and the beginning of the next.   Without discussing the composition of this picture for the present, let us merely remark that a similar pictorial moment is presented to our eyes over and over again when we watch a group of dancers on the modern stage.

If we agree, then, that there are important pictorial moments during the motions projected on the screen it is clear that the arrangement of lines, shapes, tones, and textures which impress our eyes at those moments are compositions in static forms.   And for composition in static forms we must study and apply the principles which are forever valid in painting, sculpture, and architecture.

In the production of a painting there are three main steps.   First, the painter must select his subjects. Then he must bring these subjects together and arrange them into a satisfactory composition.   Finally he must transfer his composed subject to canvas.   The same three steps must be taken in the production of a cinema picture.   The scenario writer selects the subjects and in the main plans their composition.   The director completes and executes the scenario writer's plans for the pictorial composition.   He also plans in general the results which are to obtain after the transfer has been made to the film.   The photographer, in various

[1] See page 33.

departments of his work, makes the transfer to the film.

It is an obvious advantage to the painter that he can take all three steps and go the whole distance himself, that his own personality may dominate the painting from its inception to its completion. It would be an obvious advantage to the cinema composer if he were author, director, and photographer all in one. But as long as the steps must be taken by separate persons and the distance must be covered in relays, there is an added responsibility for the scenario writer and each of the others who are concerned separately in the production of a cinema picture.

In the case of painting, the third step, the actual transfer, is the most important. It makes the greatest demands upon, and offers the greatest opportunities for, the painter's art. Any blemish of subject or short-coming of composition may be remedied in the process of putting paint on the canvas. Even after the composition of subject has been broken up, after the models have gone home, and the properties are scattered, the painter may steadily ply his brush in the third stage of production, eliminating a detail here, adding one there, subduing one effect, emphasizing another, straightening one line, bending another, deepening a shadow, intensifying a high light, blending the colours better than they were in the originals which he studied, until at last he has finished a piece of art which is beautiful because it will put the beholder into a state of contemplative satisfaction.

But any one can tell without expert knowledge that no such care can be taken, no such art exercised in the transfer, the photography, of a cinema picture. It follows, therefore, that much more care must be taken, much more art exercised in the first two steps, in the selection and composition of subjects.   A painter can turn unpromising, even ugly, subjects into beauty. The late William M. Chase could transfer a dead fish or a dozen onions into a beautiful painting.   But no such transmutation can take place in a photographic transfer.   Bad subjects are notoriously not camera proof; and bad compostion cannot be made good by the photographer after the film has been exposed, or even while the film is being exposed.

The first step, then, the selection of a subject, must be taken by the scenario writer with heavy responsibility on his shoulders and high purpose in this heart. He must supply his scenario with visually pleasant or picturesque people, in groups of three or four, or in groups of a thousand.   Whether the human subject be a hod carrier or a mediaeval prince, an Eskimo or a Hottentot, a young millionaire or a Greek galley slave, a newsboy or a cave man, a suffragette or a Harem girl, a colonial dame or a Russian queen, a " sweat shop " girl or a Roman dancer, a child at play or an old soldier in reminiscent repose, a mob of workmen " on strike," a party of hunters following the hounds, or a cavalcade of knights led by Joan of Arc — whatever the subject be, and whether it be in itself beautiful or not, it must be either pleasant or picturesque to the eye.

And since these people cannot exist in a vacuum, the scenario writer must supply them with settings, more subjects for pictures.   And whatever the setting be, whether palace or hovel, shop or club house, church or saloon, pathway or street, brook or waterfall, field or forest, mountain or sea, it, too, must satisfy the demands of beauty, not only as a thing apart, but in its function as a setting, that is, in its connection with characters and actions.

And then there are accessories to be supplied, costumes, furniture, vehicles, utensils, weapons, such things as canes and parasols, tools, toys, and animals. These, too, in their ultimate position and use must add to the beauty of the picture.

Thus for any one photoplay the materials multiply until the problem of arranging them into a pictorial composition is by no means easy of solution. It cannot be solved at all unless the subjects chosen are suitable for the composition desired. For example, let us conceive an extreme case; a Roman centurion, a skating rink, and a lady's fan may be separately pleasant or picturesque to the eye, but they do not lend themthemselves to composition, because the moment we think of them as parts of the same picture they become mutually repellent. Need we argue the matter further? It certainly must be clear by now that the primary credit and the primary blame for the pictorial value of a photoplay is due to the scenario writer; because it is he who furnishes the persons, places, things, and actions which are the substance of the picture.

Having taken the first step, having selected his subjects, the scenario writer can hardly pause. Inertia will carry him on to the second step. In fact, he would take the first step blindly, were he not planning to take the second step also. For he would be merely groping in the dark if he selected subjects at all without knowing whether he or some one else could make those subjects pictorially effective. He must take the second

step.   He must have a lively feeling for the art of pictorial composition and a general knowledge of its
principles.

The principles of composition in painting and sculpture are far more important to the cinema composer
than the finished masterpieces.   Because he can always
apply the principles in motion pictures, but he can never
successfully reproduce a famous painting or group of
statuary in motion pictures.   The man who can analyze
the construction, appeal, and effectiveness of a single
painting knows more about art than the man whose
only equipment is the possession of a thousand prints
or photographs of famous paintings.   He is a childish
and misguided enthusiast who attempts to reproduce
literally some great painting or piece of sculpture in the
motion pictures.   "Living pictures," whether at society entertainments or on the screen, may be clever,
even interesting, but they are not art; they are merely
imitations, echoes, appreciations of their originals.   To
place two peasants in the setting and pose of Millet's
"The Angelus,"[1] to drape and pose an actress like
Raphael's "The Sistine Madonna" is merely to pay a
tribute to the masterpiece imitated.   If the imitation
is well done and the beholder has an æsthetic experience, it is only because his eye sees again in memory
the inimitable beauty of the original.   No one art
can reproduce another art.   You cannot versify a
symphony or sing a cathedral.   You cannot paint
"The Venus of Milo";[2] you can only paint a representation of that statue seen from a single angle.   You
cannot cinematize a painting, nor can you paint a
cinematic picture.   But the cinema composer might do

---

[1] See page 49.   [2] See Frontispiece.

this: he might borrow the principles of the painter. He might some time, without imitating " The Angelus," produce a pictorial moment in a photoplay which was characterized by the same simplicity and reverent repose of subject, the same low key and gradation of tones, the same appeal to the auditory imagination, a pictorial moment which would give us contemplative satisfaction and would impress us as original because it did not remind us of any other piece of art.

Before proceeding to an analytic discussion of pictorial composition for the screen let us first understand the special conditions under which such composition must be made.   In the first place the beholders of a motion picture, no matter when looking, or in how large a company, all have the same single point of view.   They all see the picture with a single eye, the lens of the camera.   Similarly all of the beholders of a painting have the same point of view.   But no such condition prevails in viewing any given grouping, any given picture in the stage drama.   Take, for example, the moment in the trial scene of *The Merchant of Venice* when Portia has just cried out " Tarry a little," thus arresting the gesture of Shylock, who was about to bury his knife in the bosom of Antonio.   The stage director has arranged a dozen people in a particular grouping to emphasize pictorially the tragic import of the action.   But the composition is not the same to any two people in the theatre.   The spectator in the second balcony looks down upon the heads of the actors, and the spectator in the orchestra looks up beneath their chins.   The spectator in the left hand stage box sees Shylock standing between him and Antonio and the spectator to the right of the centre aisle sees them standing side by side. The philosophic stage director, therefore, must always group any particular stage picture for sculpturesque effects, that is, for effects that are equally expressive from the hundreds of angles within a very large arc of vision. But the motion picture director, like the painter, can arrange his subject for a single effect, and record the composition permanently to be seen by all with a single eye. This means that he can work for the utmost subtlety of line and tonal gradation, the utmost cohesion between figures, the utmost dramatic significance of the pictorial group.

Another condition of the motion picture is that it must practically always fill a rectangular frame of unvarying shape. This is so because the film has been standardized so that every separate exposure fills a frame of fixed proportions. The painter has no such limitation; nor have you when you carry your kodak. You may, for example, turn your kodak over on its side, thus making your picture higher than it is wide. Or, after the negative has been developed, you may print your picture and trim it down to any shape, making it square, round, or elliptical. In exceptional cases the motion picture may depart from the standard dimensions, as when some masking device is used to shut out partially or frame in the subject. But in the vast majority of cases the standard rectangular frame must be used, whether the subject be a kitten or a herd of buffaloes. Either subject may fill the frame. In the theatre of the spoken drama a similar fixed frame conditions the stage picture. In recent years producers have made attempts to escape the unvarying height and breadth of the proscenium arch by virtually building a stage within the stage, a device, by the way, which dates back to Shakespeare. This reduction of the picture frame is accomplished by masking the theatre stage down to a desired size, as in Granville Barker's production of *The Man Who Married a Dumb Wife,* or by throwing all except the desired portion of the stage into darkness, as in Barrie's *A Kiss for Cinderella.* Yet the limitation of the fixed frame cannot be entirely overcome by the stage director, because the visual range of exhibition is also fixed. He cannot bring a locket or a seal ring near enough to the audience for inspection, and he cannot put the departing regiment far enough away for the best pictorial and emotional effect. But the photoplay director may make his picture small enough for the smallest subject and large enough for the largest. He may compose a picture of a woman's fingers plucking the petals from a daisy, or of four thousand warriors storming the walls of Babylon. He may even, if necessary, photograph microscopic life, thus presenting objects that are too small to be seen with the naked eye. This tremendous range in vision and flexibility of frame are, as we shall see, invaluable resources to the cinema composer in producing pictorial value, as well as dramatic value, of his subject and composition.

At present the use of colour is, perhaps fortunately, not practical in the motion pictures. But there is a great resource of tonal value in the blackest black, the whitest white, and all the subtle gradations lying in between. There is also an infinite range of intensity, from the shadowy ghost so thin and airy that it can scarcely be seen, to the sharp reality of the two edged

sword or the 42 centimeter cannon. This varying of intensity is, of course, made possible by a
mechanical device of photography, that is, the regula-
tion of the light, not upon the subject, but within the
camera.   But the artificial lighting of the subject also
conditions the composition of the motion picture.   For
example, a good silhouette picture can be much more
easily produced on the screen than on the stage of the
spoken drama.

All of these conditions of pictorial effect on the
screen, the single viewpoint, the constant frame, the
choice of distance, the range in tonal value, the range
in intensity, the possibilities of artificial lighting and
camera magic, should be kept in mind by the scenario
writer.   He should miss no opportunity for a new
appeal to the eye; and he will surely find, as sculptors,
painters, musicians have found, that a limitation may
itself be an opportunity.

Under certain rules of the game, so to speak, the
cinema composer proceeds to arrange his material, his
persons, places, things, and actions into a composition.
But how is he to know that a certain arrangement is a
good composition and that a dozen other arrangements
of the same subjects are bad composition?   Shall he
merely shuffle his materials thirteen times and pick out
the best arrangement that chance has produced?   If he
tries leaving the whole matter to the god of chance he
will find that even a hundred shufflings might not produce a single composition satisfactory to the eye.   No,
he must arrange his materials deliberately, purposely,
carefully.   He must know before he begins his task
that certain principles intelligently applied will produce
the effect he desires.

These principles of pictorial composition are: unity, emphasis, balance, and rhythm.   And all of these principles have reference to the lines, or shapes, the tones, the textures, and, of course, to the character, or significance, of the subjects.

Unity of significance is the first essential when persons, places, and things are brought together.   We cannot compose a picture of the Roman centurion, the skating rink, and the lady's fan, because those three subjects have no common significance.   We cannot think of them as mutually expressing a single idea. Common sense will usually tell the scenario writer what persons and things have a unity of significance.   But, judging by the pictures we see on the screen, the mandates of common sense are distressingly weak when it comes to the question of properly relating setting to persons and actions.   The proper use of setting with respect to dramatic significance is a question of such importance that we shall defer its discussion to a separate chapter.

But unity of significance, though necessary, is not enough.   The subjects must also lend themselves to unified treatment of line and tone.   Suppose our scenario calls for an artist's studio containing the artist himself in a painter's frock, an easel, palette and brushes, a Louis XIV chair, a rustic bench, a Chinese pitcher, and two or three canvases turned to the wall.   All of these things have obvious unity of significance; and yet, though we could represent such a subject, we could not turn it into a satisfactory picture, because the various parts of the picture would not harmonize in shape and tone.

A frequent violation of unity results when some

From *The Scarlet Woman*. [...] [...]

From *The Scarlet Woman*. This composition lacks unity because the conspicuous line of the portiere separates it into two distinct parts. See page 43.

strong line divides the picture into two parts. We have before us a " still " from the Metro photoplay, *The Scarlet Woman.*[1] The picture shows three people in a reception room. Observing from left to right we see a man evidently arguing with another man, a portière in strong light extending from the top to the bottom of the picture, and a woman standing on the first step of a stair case. The composition is bad because the conspicuous line of the portière divides the picture into separate parts, as separate as if there were two separate rooms.

It is sometimes desirable to show more than one locale simultaneously, and two or more locales can be so arranged that they possess pictorial unity. Here is a " still " from the Lasky *Carmen.*[2] In the foreground is the large room of a Spanish tavern. Just beyond the area is the wide, dark archway through another wing of the building. And beyond the archway can be seen a section of Spanish landscape stretching to the horizon. We have therefore four separate locales presented simultaneously, and yet we do not think of them as four separate pictures. The director has recognized his opportunity of composing in depth, or distance, and his four locales, being separated by nothing but air, fall together into a single composition. Imagine a comparison between this composition of locales and a scene from a photoplay entitled *The Hand of Peril,* in which the director prided himself on presenting a cross section of an apartment house with action going on in nine rooms simultaneously. The nine-room cross section did not, of course, look like a picture at all, but rather like a plumber's advertisement.

[1] See page 42.   [2] See page 149.

As soon as we are sure that our subjects when properly composed will possess the quality of unity, we may turn our attention to the question of emphasis. There is a double necessity for emphasis. It is necessary to indicate to the beholder the central theme, significance, or purpose of the picture. And it is necessary to focalize the attention of the eye somewhere, to give it a chance to rest somewhere in its inspection of the picture. Emphasis is further necessary to produce unity. There is no real unity in a handful of sand, because the grains of sand are all alike. No one grain is more important than another. There is no interdependence or subordination, and consequently no cohesion and unity. But there is unity, because there is emphasis, in a hand holding a handful of sand; because the sand is obviously subordinate to the hand. Thus there is emphasis in Rodin's piece of sculpture, " The Hand of God," because everything the hand holds is subordinate to the hand itself. Pictorial emphasis may be produced by significance, by position, by shape, and by tonal value or lighting.

A subject is emphasized by position when it is given an isolated, yet dominating place, a place toward which other lines of interest converge. In Raphael's painting, " The Sistine Madonna," the Madonna is emphasized by her position at the apex of a triangle. In a photograph of the Alps from Interlaken, Die Jungfrau is emphasized to the eye because it is the highest point on the horizon, and because all the lines of the landscape lead up to its summit. In a photograph of the Yale football team running out upon the gridiron the captain is emphasized by his position at the head of the team. To illustrate the lack of emphasis let us select a

From *Audrey*. The composition lacks definite pictorial emphasis. Neither lines, tonal value, position, nor gesture are employed to centralize our attention on the heroine. See pages 45, 46.

" still " from the Famous Players' photoplay, *Audrey*.[1]
The subject is a congregation of about fifty people in a
country church.   The picture is entitled " While Others
Prayed," and evidently means that while others were
praying, some one, perhaps Audrey, was not.   But it
is necessary to inspect the picture for some time before
we find Audrey.   Puzzle!   Ah, there she is in the
middle of the fifth pew on the right hand side.   No
wonder it was so hard to find her.   She is in no way
accented by position; no lines help to guide our eye
to her place.   If in that whole congregation hers had
been the only head not bowed, her position would have
been isolated and we could have found her in a flash.

An object is emphasized by shape when the lines
which define or characterize its shape are more unfamiliar, interesting, or striking than any other lines
in the picture.   Here in a " still " from the Metro
photoplay, *What Will People Say?* is an example of
emphasis misplaced because of shapes that strike the
eye.[2]   The subject is two men and a woman in a pre-
tentious room of some kind.   There are two large
windows with conspicuous grill work silhouetted darkly
against the sky.   The grill work is so fantastic in design that our eyes find no interest in the human figures
of the tableau.   For a contrast to this let us look again
at Millet's " The Angelus." [3]   Here, although no lines
are very conspicuous, the most interesting ones are
those which bound the head and shoulders of the young
woman.   The shape and pose of her head silhouetted
against the sky emphasize her as a symbol of reverent
peasantry.

[1] See page 45.   [2] See page 42.   [3] See page 49.

Emphasis may finally be secured by lighting or tonal value of the subject. It is an optical law that the eye when inspecting a picture seeks and rests upon the highest white, the deepest black, or the strongest contrast in tone.[1] Thus Napoleon is easily found in Meissonier's painting, " Friedland 1807," because he is centrally placed on a white horse, with no other white object near him. In the Metro " still," just referred to, our eyes clung to the fantastic grill work, partly because of the striking design, as we have just said; but partly also because of the tonal contrast between the black metal work and bright sky. In the Famous Players' " still " of *Audrey* the heroine would have been discovered immediately if she had been the only one wearing a white dress and hat. In Millet's " The Angelus " there is a strong light on the woman's dress, which helps to make her more prominent than the other figure in the painting. The motion picture director, as we have said above, has larger possibilities than the stage director in controlling the lighting of his subject. But he must be extremely careful in trying to realize these opportunities. He must remember that black may be as emphatic as white, and that a sharp contrast may lead the eye away from the focal interest of the picture. Furthermore he must remember that the best emphasis of all is secured when tonal value co-operates with position and shape to mark the dramatic significance and to produce pictorial unity and repose. It would be unpardonable stupidity to give a wrong emphasis by all of these principles of composition. Yet that is exactly what was done at one of the pictorial moments of the Famous Players' photoplay, *Diplo-*

[1] See page 47.

From *Diplomacy*. It is hard to believe that even accident could produce so bad a composition. Cover the lion completely with your fingers and you will see the dramatic expression which was really intended. See page 46.

From *The Masked Rider*. Emphasis is produced by tonal isolation (white), by line (arm and legs serving as radii to focalize optical attention), by position in group, and by significance of gesture. The composition also has unity, balance, and rhythm. See page 46.

macy.[1] The " still " shows a man and woman standing about four feet apart, with a stone lion directly between them and about a foot behind the plane in which they are standing. The lion is of no significance whatever, either dramatically or pictorially. Yet this lion is emphatic, first, because it is the largest white mass in the picture; second, because of its striking pose, its fantastic mane of a kind never seen in the jungle, and its facial expression such as only a stone lion can wear; and, third, because it is so placed between the two people that when the man shakes his finger at the woman he seems to be shaking his finger at the startled lion. It is hard to believe that even accident could produce so bad a composition.

While a good picture must have unity and emphasis, it must also have balance; balance of subject, of line, and of tone. To begin with, the subjects themselves must be in equilibrium. If they are not, the beholder, feeling the lack of repose, fails to get into a state of contemplative satisfaction. We do not want to feel that the discus thrower is going to fall down either before or after he throws the discus, that one of the muses is going to trip at the next step in the dance, or that the woman in " The Angelus " is so prayerful that she is falling over forwards. Equilibrium must obtain also in the picture as a composition. We must not feel that one side of the group is too heavy for the other, or that the top is too heavy for the bottom. In this connection it must be remembered that balance is not always a matter of pounds. It may be rather a matter of interest, of dramatic significance. A lanky sheriff on one side of the picture may be in perfect bal-

[1] See page 47.

ance with a mob of a hundred men on the other side of the picture. Another thing of special interest to the cinema composer is that balance can be obtained through the depth of the picture, that is, that something in the distance can be placed in pictorial equilibrium with something near the camera. Thus in " The Angelus " the chapel dimly seen in the distance balances the two figures and three objects in the foreground.

Another thing, not so obvious as balance of subject, is what might be called optical balance, or balance of line and tone. The eye sweeps over a picture more quickly than thought, up and down, backward and forward, and around the whole composition. The tour may be repeated over and over again during a second of time. If every single line and tone seen in this tour is totally different from every other line and tone, then the eye must constantly adjust itself to a new optical sensation, and naturally grows weary in the process, however quick it may be. But if the eye finds one line repeating or echoing another line, one tone repeating or echoing another, then it finds occasional rest in its tour and the pleasure of familiar acquaintance, somewhat like our pleasure in travelling when we meet an old friend, even though he has changed a bit since last we saw him.

Let us test some of these theories of balance by considering the letters of the alphabet as compositions in line. Testing for balance of subject, or substance, we see that A, H, K, M, R, W, and X have better balance than F, P, or V. There is better unity in A or X than in H, which exhibits a tendency to fall into halves despite the cross bar. Now if we look for balance of

THE ANGELUS
See Index

line, we see that S, though its equilibrium is none too sure, is satisfactory to the eye, because the lower half of the figure is a repetition with variation of the upper half. In the letters W and X we find a mathematically perfect balance of lines and angles, but their balance is too perfect, too severe to be pictorially satisfactory. Perhaps, without arguing the matter further, we may lay down the principle, that the eye is more pleased by repetition with variation than with absolute repetition. We have said that the eye becomes wearied when it must continuously experience new sensations; we now add that the eye also grows wearied by the monotony of continuous perfect repetition.

The principle of repetition with variation operates beautifully in " The Angelus." There is parallelism of verticals and horizontals, but the parallels are not absolutely perfect, and the angles of the crossing lines are not absolutely equal angles. Note the verticals in the standing figures, the potato fork, and the distant spire. Note the horizontals in the horizon, the potato rows, and the handles of the wheelbarrow. The lines are balanced, but not as formally perfect as if arranged by the aid of a level and plumb line. When we examine the circular lines of the design we see that here too there is balance, though not absolute repetition. Note the curved lines of the woman's head, the man's head, the basket, the wheel of the wheelbarrow, and the fold of the woman's skirt. These lines are not drawn with the aid of a pair of compasses. If we turn to another design, " Apollo and the Muses," [1] mentioned above, we see that oblique lines are prominent. Select any line in the bodies or draperies of the dancers,

[1] See page 33.

and it will be found roughly paralleled by some balancing line in the composition.

One might think at first that balance of line is no immediate concern of the scenario writer who cannot direct his own play.   But the moment a scenario writer specifies a particular person in a particular place he concerns himself with the question of pictorial composition in lines.   If the lines of the place cannot be made to harmonize with that figure or costume, the scenario writer is at fault.   The moment he introduces additional figures and an object or two, he has still further complicated the problem of composition, and he must bear the blame if the subjects he has specified cannot be composed into a pictorial harmony.

In addition to balance of subject and balance of lines a pictorial composition must also have balance of tones. In a painting such balance is usually perceived in terms of colour.   Thus a bit of red in a costume may be echoed by another bit of red in the room, in a rug, in a piece of bric-a-brac, or in a picture on the wall.   Or the same red may be balanced in another way by its complementary colour green.   When such a painting is photographed the colour, or what we call colour, disappears, but the tonal value remains, and in a good painting remains in balance.   In this connection let us quote a paragraph from Vachel Lindsay's " *The Art of the Moving Picture* ": " Some people do not consider that photographic black, white, and grey are colour.   But here for instance are seven colours which the Imagists might use :   (1) The whiteness of swans in the light.   (2) The whiteness of swans in a gentle shadow.   (3) The colour of a sunburned man in the light.   (4) His colour in a gentle shadow.   (5) His colour in a deeper shadow. (6) The blackness of black velvet in the light. (7) The blackness of black velvet in a deep shadow. And to use these colours with definite steps from one to the other does not militate against an artistic mystery of edge and softness in the flow of line. There is a list of possible Imagist textures which is only limited by the number of things to be seen in the world."

It is easy to imagine the differences in tonal value of the subjects named by Mr. Lindsay; and it is just as easy to perceive the differences in tonal value in a photograph or print of a painting. In the print of " The Angelus " we observe that the whitest light is in the woman's skirt just beneath her arm. This tone is balanced on the right hand side of the picture by the light on the potato sacks, the glint of light on the lower edge of the wheel, and the light caught by the lower corner of her apron. It is balanced on the left hand side by the white of the man's shirt, the tip of light on the handle of the potato fork, and the rim of light on the edge of the basket. A further analysis of the picture reveals the fact that the blacks and greys are distributed and balanced in the same way.

The tonal value of the motion picture is determined by two factors: the material surface or texture of the body, costume, object, or setting, and the kind and amount of light falling upon such surface or texture. Does the scenario writer see where his chief responsibility lies? Does the director realize that even in outdoor subjects it might be worth while to wait until the sun is in the right quarter, to erect artificial shades or reflectors, if necessary, and to seek until he finds the best position of the camera?

The fourth quality which may be produced, or looked for, in a picture is the quality of rhythm, rhythm in line and in tone. Rhythm is primarily thought of in connection with fluent forms, but it may also be thought of as operating in static forms. For although the movement is not in the picture, it is in the eye which observes the picture. The eye, as we have said, makes a tour of inspection. If in this tour of inspection it has consecutive sensations which repeat themselves with variation, the effect on the eye is rhythmical. We have already used much the same terms in defining balance, but it must be remembered that balance implies the equilibrium of only two units, that is, only one repetition, while in rhythm we usually think of more than one repetition. An important condition of rhythm is that the repetition must not be mathematical. When, for example, your clock strikes twelve you hear a series of sounds of equal duration, and equally far apart; but the effect is not rhythmical. But a proper alteration of the duration, pitch, or quality of some of these sounds would produce rhythm. If by the aid of a ruler and a square you draw a zig-zag line across the page, making every angle a right angle and every "leg" of the line exactly one inch long, the effect on the eye would not be rhythmical. Or if with the aid of compasses you draw a meandering line in which all the curves repeat the arc of the same circle the result is not rhythmical. But turn to a photograph or print of the "Venus of Milo," [1] preferably the view from a point directly in front of the statue; in inspecting this composition your eye will travel over many rhythmical lines. Begin, for

[1] See Frontispiece.

example, at the right side of her head and follow the sinuous, varying curves over her right shoulder down the side of her body to her right foot. This entire line taken as a whole is a rhythmical line. It harmonizes with two other rhythmical lines, one extending down the left side of her body, and one beginning with her nose and extending down the centre of her body. The eye enjoys following these lines because they seem to flow as easily and as pleasingly as the undulations of the sea. The pleasure is instinctive; it is there whether the beholder is able to analyze it or not.

The director who wishes to mark a rhythmical line here and there in his composition must train his eye until he instinctively sees a rhythmical line before he composes it. If he cannot invent a beautiful line of his own let him borrow from the inexhaustible wealth of nature. If he is grouping a crowd let him cut its fringe like the edge of a curving sea beach; let him file a row of tourists over a glacier like a meandering brook or an old road winding down a valley; let him pattern his draperies from the drooping branches of the willow; let him learn how to transfer to his compositions the rhythms which may be found in the sweeping horizon of the foothills, in the billowy boundaries of a summer cloud, in the trailing smoke of a river steamboat, in the elegant back of a thoroughbred horse or greyhound.

Tonal rhythm, like linear rhythm, involves repetition with variation, and is an extension of the principle of tonal balance. Suppose we group five girls in a straight row, the middle girl wearing a black dress, the girls next to her on either side wearing white dresses, and the girls at either end of the row wearing black dresses. We have then the tonal pattern, black, white, black, white, black. This is mathematical balance, but not rhythm. Suppose now that we change the costumes and get this order of values: dark grey, white, dark grey, light grey, black. Whether that result is the best rhythm or not, it certainly is more rhythmical than the result of the first arrangement. We see now that tonal rhythm also involves soft half tones and subtle gradations. The contrast between black and white placed sharply together is like the acute angle of two lines; the difference between light grey meeting dark grey is more like an obtuse angle; and the grading of two neighbouring tones until they blend softly is like wearing down an angle until it becomes an easy curve.

For the sake of clearness we have discussed four principles of pictorial composition in separate sections of this chapter; but this does not mean that the scenario writer or director should apply them separately at different hours or on different days of his work, or that they operate separately upon the eye of the beholder. There must be a single harmony of unity, emphasis, balance, and rhythm. There must be a totality of result and a simultaneity of appeal to the eye. Are we not discussing a pictorial moment, a flash, rather than a pictorial permanence on canvas or paper? Perhaps at this point some sceptic, a man of action and not of theories, may say " That's just it. The grouping at that moment is only a flash anyway. Why should I worry my head about such high-falutin ideas as balance or rhythm? If a picture isn't perfect we can get away with it all right.

The crowd won't have time to notice the defect."
Our reply is simply this: The director who is satisfied to "get away with it" is not going forward, he
is not developing, he will never help to elevate the
cinema play from "movies" to art.   But, to get back
to the main question, the briefer the pictorial moment
is, the more important it is that its unity and emphasis
shall help us to grasp the central significance immediately, and that our eyes shall not be distracted by
ugly lines or lack of balance.   Therefore the man who
believes that physical laws of sight and visual perception govern pictorial composition, as the laws of sound
govern musical composition, and believes that action
should be controlled by thought and not by accident,
will welcome and test any theory which aims to make
the photoplay most effective.   Such a seeker for effi-
ciency in art should supplement our brief discussion
by reading, for example, Henry R. Poore's *Pictorial
Composition (Eleventh Edition, Revised)*, or C. W.
Valentine's *Experimental Psychology of Beauty,*
should study the designs of painting and sculpture
in every art gallery he can visit, should study Nature
herself, and should watch the screen for the failures
as well as the triumphs of those who are at present
producing photoplays.   If the seeker can discover new
laws of nature he will go down in his history as a
scientist; if he can apply old laws to new problems,
and can make new combinations of beauty he will
forever be remembered as an artist.   We have been
enthusiastic about the application of the principles
of pictorial composition to the photoplay because
we realize that, as Mr. Poore puts it, "In whatsoever
degree more of the *man* and less of the *mechanics*

appear, *in that degree* is the result a work of art."
We insist that, although the man has little opportunity
for expression of his own individuality in the execu-
tion, that is, in the filming and projection of a photoplay, he has most alluring opportunity for expressing
himself in the selection and composition of subjects
to be filmed and projected.

But in our enthusiasm we must not forget that
pictorial appeals are after all only the language of
the cinema composer, as words are the language of
the novelist. All euphony of word and cadence of
sentence is in vain unless they help the writer to convey and emphasize the thought he has to express.
And all pictorial appeal is in vain unless it in some
way contributes to the dramatic significance in the
photoplay. We must remember that the pictorial moment is not isolated in its function. It is dependent
and co-operative. It is a small but organic part in a
large whole. Suppose we are representing a rough-
and-tumble fight lasting four or five minutes. The
dominating note is struggle and chaos. It would be
bad art to produce in the midst of this fight a pictorial
moment of rhythmical repose. Tragedy may sometime demand ugliness, and comedy may sometime demand unstable equilibrium. Furthermore, it is not
possible that all exposures of the camera should record
beautiful pictures. In literature, even in a beautiful
poem, there may be such words as " or," " if," " the,"
" as," etc., which, though not in themselves beautiful,
contribute to the total beauty of the literary work.
So in the photoplay some of the items may be close-
ups of unpictorial things, such as a bunch of keys, a
pocket knife, or a newspaper clipping; yet these mere

representations, not pictures, are necessary for the total value of the photoplay.

The pure pictures of a photoplay may be classified as merely decorative pictures, portraits, and dramatic tableaux. The merely decorative picture is a strong temptation to the inartistic producer. The director on his way to a " location " demanded in the scenario happens to see a flock of sheep. Now the scenario does not call for any flock of sheep, nor would a flock of sheep help to interpret or enforce any message of that scenario. But this is such a good-looking flock of sheep! It would be a pity not to film it for the delectation of five hundred thousand " movie " fans. So out comes the camera, and in goes the innocent flock of sheep. Not very long ago a producer spent a million dollars, or said that he did, in producing an enormous collection, a veritable museum, of pictorial effects, of which easily eighty percent were detachable decorations of the plot. That photoplay included many " sure fire " pictures, from the dashing waves to the coiling smoke over a burning village, from kittens to swans, from flowers to palm trees, from cunning babies to cruel witches, from naked diving girls to heroic warriors in fantastic panoply, yet the total result was in no way memorable, except as a disgusting misdirection of artistic resources, and as a deservedly bad investment of money. Now if only five percent of these pictures had been merely decorative, and the other ninety-five percent had been dramatic tableaux or portrait delineations of character, the film would certainly have had more value as a piece of art. The preceding statement is an admission that an occasional merely decorative picture may have a place in a photoplay. Shakespeare often introduced comic relief during a dramatic pause in some grim tragedy. In the same way the cinema composer may sometime introduce pictorial relief, something to rest the eye and quiet the emotions after a dramatic crisis. We may even go so far as to say that pictorial beauty might well be used to compensate those portions of a plot where dramatic suspense and acting value is low. In other words, when you cannot appeal to the mind of the spectator, by all means appeal to his eye.

But the highest achievement of a screen portrait is the delineation of human character. Pose, grouping, setting, composition of line and colour are all in vain if they do not reveal to us the interesting personality of the subject. All those pictorial values are but the language of the artist with which he describes his character. In the photoplay human personality is delineated partly by the actor and partly by the art of the director who composes persons, places, and things into portrait pictures. We shall discuss the delineation of character and the dramatization of setting in later chapters of this book.

The photoplay must not only portray human characters, but it must portray human characters in action, that is, in dramatic action. Frequently in this action comes a crisis, and ultimately comes a climax. These intense moments must, in the highest cinema art, be represented pictorially by dramatic tableaux, and not by printed words thrown upon the screen. Vachel Lindsay puts the matter well. " The climax of a motion picture scene cannot be one word or fifty words. As has been discussed in connection with

Cabiria, the crisis must be an action sharper than any that has gone before in organic union with a tableau more beautiful than any that has preceded: the breaking of the tenth wave upon the sand." Let us define a dramatic tableau as the picture in which the greatest number of dramatic values can be visually grasped in a single moment. It is most intense in the visible representation of a conflict, a struggle, physical or mental, or both. The director in composing this tableau must remember that the dramatic meaning should be read in every part of the picture, in the setting, the furniture, the things, the grouping, the lines, the tones, as well as in the face of the chief performer. Breadth, completeness, pictorial totality must never be sacrificed to the ambition or vanity of " a star."

If the spectator sitting in a motion picture theatre can be placed in intimate contact with an interesting personality, can be placed in sympathetic suspense concerning a human struggle, and can be given emotional satisfaction by the outcome of that struggle, then the pictorial delineation and narration which produced those results may be considered good art. But it is by no means necessary that the spectator shall be aware of the pictorial methods responsible for the result. He need not be conscious of the fact that the particular picture was beautiful because it had no jarring note, no disagreeable subject, no bad balance, no ugly lines, or that the meaning of the particular picture was made clear and impressive through unity and emphasis. He need not even be subconscious of the principles of pictorial composition. But the cinema composer will have to understand, obey, and apply those principles consciously until he can understand, obey, and apply them subconsciously, until in fact they become second nature to him.

Thus we have made a systematic analysis of the principles of pictorial composition in static forms, because such forms are present even in the motion picture. But the pictorial moments are after all only incidents in the pictorial movement. They must emphasize without retarding, they must stress without stopping the cinematic movement. And since this movement also must be effectively composed, we turn next to a chapter on pictorial composition in fluent forms.

CHAPTER IV

It has been maintained in the previous chapter that the pictorial values in the ideal photoplay should be so arranged that, if the action were suddenly arrested at any one of the pictorial moments which the play must contain, the resulting " still " would be considered beautiful according to the same standards which we habitually apply to paintings. This requirement of artistic composition depends upon our proposition that in a great many pictured actions certain pictorial instants, or moments, are more impressive and longer remembered than the pictorial movement. Now, without contradicting what has been said, we shall show that many subjects in nature and in mobile arts are more beautiful and memorable in motion than in repose, and that therefore the accomplished cinema composer must be able to select and compose his motions as effectively as his " stills."

His schooling will begin with contemplation of the dance and pantomime, ancient arts employing essentially the beauty and expressiveness of human movement. He will draw inspiration from gazing at the fascinating movement of bird and beast and fish, of tree and cloud and wave, movement which none of the older arts can present. He will observe how painter and sculptor have for centuries struggled with the problem of merely suggesting, not representing, movement by a medium in repose, and he will feel his full responsibility and glimpse his large reward when he realizes that now for the first time in history it has become possible to capture and mobilize in art any movement which the human eye can perceive, and movements even which the unaided eye cannot perceive.

It may be edifying to see in what cases the movement of a subject is more beautiful or appealing than the repose of the same subject. Take, for example, the simple figure of a circle. Which is more appealing to the eye, the child's hoop rolling over the turf, or the same hoop held still in the child's hand or lying on the grass? The whirling circle which a child describes with a glowing brand, or any fixed circle, say a gold ring? The moving circle has a fundamental appeal in the child's game as well as in the art of the dancer. For this reason Giulio Romano was not content to let his Apollo and the Muses stand in a circle; they must seem to move in a circle. Now let us consider a pattern of static circles having a common centre, as, for example, the design on a button. No such fixed arrangement of circles can ever be so mysteriously fascinating as the moving pattern on the surface of a pool where a pebble has just gone down. Whatever the explanation may be, it is true that the baby and the grandmother alike gaze with pleased expression at the rings rising from a fixed centre, chasing each other in all directions until they vanish in the vain pursuit. No such pleasure to the eye could ever come from an instantaneous photograph of the same pattern. An allied effect may be produced by circles contracting about a common centre, a phenomenon which may be observed by a passenger on the rear platform of a tube train as he gazes into the receding tunnel.   Such a phenomenon, too, is the vortex of water where the lines rush spirally downward toward a vanishing point.   If it is true that these effects are more beautiful in movement than in repose, the cinema composer is happy in being able to represent them cinematically.

But he should go further.   He should transfer these fundamental principles of visual appeal to any photoplay subject where they may possibly apply. The moving circle, for example, may be applied to games, dancing, military manœuvres, groups of animals, etc., always producing a result which is pictorial to the eye.   The curving lines of the rushing Niagara may be transferred to a crowd pouring out of a building.   The leaping, flaring lines of the surf breaking on a rock may be utilized by a group of dancing girls waving their scarves; and the radiating lines of a sky rocket may reappear in a troop of soldiers deploying up a gently sloping hill.   The undulating lines of a ribbon rippling in the breeze may, in retarded tempo, characterize a herd of sheep filing down a mountain path, or the battle front of an army swaying beneath the attack of the enemy.   The photoplay director may represent these optical effects as he finds them in nature or familiar life, or he may transfer them, as has been suggested, or he may utilize the same effect in two different subjects simultaneously, thus harmonizing his values.   The girls may dance in the presence of the surf; the troops may deploy beneath sky rockets.

There are many cases where the instantaneous photograph is not nearly so effective as the picture in motion.   One of the earliest subjects of the cinematograph was the railway train, first appearing as a tiny speck in the distance, then gradually expanding in size until it bore down upon the beholder with a rushing reality that made him almost feel the suction of the air wash.   Whether the train was going or coming the moving pattern of converging or diverging perspective made an impression on the eye which could never be suggested in painting or adequately described in words.   Such a moving pattern is a unique element in the hands of the cinema composer which he should fit into artistic union with the rest of his composition in fluent forms.   He should do more; he should harmonize his pictured motion with the meaning of the play.   Thus the approaching train might somehow create the impression of climax, of culmination, and the train vanishing into the horizon might symbolize the sadness of farewell.

Turning from the consideration of lines, curved or straight, in motion we may find equally beautiful phenomena in the plane in motion.   The undulating surface of the sea, and the billowy plane of a wheatfield in a June breeze suggest optical effects which might be utilized in a group of dancers or, in a less formal way, in the mob of the market place.   Moving textures, too, should be studied for their cinematic effect; because the cinematograph alone can transmit the charm of the changing pattern of falling snow, the calm majesty of ice floes drifting down the river, the dark sheen of coiling smoke, or the image-weaving magic of summer clouds.   Such phenomena should appear when appropriate in the photoplay as well as in the travel picture, and the principles of their appeal to the eye should be kept in mind by the director when costuming and handling his dramatic crowds.

The movement of tone, that is, the gradual changing from dark to bright, from dim to distinct, and vice versa, has already been much exploited by the photoplay director. The typical "fade-in" and "fade-out" when properly done is undoubtedly pleasing to the eye. But this changing of tone would be much more subtle in its effect if it could be accompanied by a changing of pattern. One of the natural beauties eternally unattainable by painters is the colour play of the sun setting behind a fleecy web of clouds. Why is it that the colourists of the brush are never able to represent a sunset with beauty and conviction? Simply because the optical values consist in the gradual, subtle changing of tint and pattern rather than in the static arrangement at any given moment. To take another example, what painter could ever convey the delicate impression our eyes get from the sudden fading of the glow in the wake of a meteor? Pictorial values of motion such as these admittedly defy the cinematograph too, a defiance, however, which only emphasizes our general contention that there is a whole realm of beauty which exists in fluent, though not in static, form, and can be transmitted by art only when the fluent form is reproduced.

To transmit this fluent beauty is the mission of the cinema composer. His task, though inviting, is difficult, for he is the pioneer in this new field of art. First he must have an eye to the proper composition of the movements which lie between the beginning and end of any one scene. Mr. Cecil de Mille, of the Lasky studios, has done good work in the composition within scenes. In *Joan, the Woman,* for example, the grouping and transition within a given scene was so directed that successive rearrangements of figures with reference to the setting made a succession of groupings which individually satisfied the demands of rhythm and balance in pictorial composition.

But the composition of motion values within a scene is merely the first and easy part of the general problem of composition of fluent forms. The crux of the problem is the organization of separate and seemingly unrelated motions into a totality characterized by unity, emphasis, balance, and rhythm. Could you, for example, arrange the rolling hoop, the whirling brand, the vortex, the water fall, the surf, the sky rocket, the ribbon, the train, the sea, the wheat field, the falling snow, the drifting ice floes, the coiling smoke, the clouds, the meteor, and the sunset into a single satisfactory composition? Which element would you put first, which third or seventh, which last? Which elements would you reject, which emphasize? If you were asked to project five given colours upon a screen in succession, in what order would you project them to produce the most pleasing effect upon the eye? A five reel photoplay contains hundreds of different exposures of action laid in fifty or a hundred different settings. Now if the photoplay is to be looked upon as art it follows that all its various parts must be assembled and joined in such a fashion that the complete composition will give continuous pleasure to the eye from beginning to the end of the exhibition. And this fluent pictorial value must, of course, be co-ordinated with the dramatic meaning of the play.

It is clearly evident that composition of motion pictures is an entirely different thing from composition in painting or photography, in sculpture or architecture.   The visible stimuli in those arts do not vanish while you look at them.   They are there as long as you look, will be there tomorrow, and will remain constantly present to the eye as long as the art object endures.   But the motion picture is an ever originating series of ever vanishing aspects.   And the composition of the photoplay is a combination of no-longer-seen pictures with being-seen pictures with not-yet-seen pictures.   In other words, the cinematic composition appeals simultaneously to the memory, the perception, and the expectation of the beholder.   Hence it is analogous to musical composition, the arrangement of ever originating, ever vanishing sounds.   In listening to music the ear, so to speak, remembers, hears, and expects, just as in seeing a photoplay the eye, so to speak, remembers, sees, and expects.   It is to music therefore that the cinema composer may turn for his principles of composition in fluent forms.

The analogy between sounds in a series and sights or visibles in a series is perfect.   Either has duration, rate, and tone quality.   A picture may have intensity or sharpness as a note has stress, and its tones or colours may be arranged in a high or low key just as notes may be arranged in a high or low key.   A number of notes struck simultaneously may constitute a chord just as a number of colours or graphic values represented simultaneously may constitute a static picture.   A succession of notes is not beautiful unless it possesses rhythm or melody; so a succession of visible stimuli is not beautiful to the eye unless it, too, possesses some kind of rhythm or harmony. When we listen to music the notes which have just died away into silence are still vividly present in memory and have an organic connection with the notes which are yet to come. So the pictorial values which have just faded out of sight are still present in memory and affect our appreciation of the pictorial values that follow them. It could even be shown by practical tests in a psychological laboratory that the eye, having seen part of a given sequence of pictorial values is in suspense, or, so to speak, experiences expectation for the rest of the sequence and would be shocked if what followed were inharmonious in design, tone, or colour; just as any one can prove to himself by listening to music that when part of a sequence or phrase has been played, the ear, so to speak, expects or is attuned to the complementary notes which will round out the rhythm or melody.

Hence it must be clear that any photoplay director who looks upon himself as an artist rather than a drill master, who desires some day to produce a photoplay which shall be known as a classic, must learn to compose his fluent forms, must learn to apply the principles of unity, emphasis, balance, and rhythm to the ever vanishing, ever originating visible values which he projects upon the screen. He will find this a difficult ideal to realize, because, unlike the musician, he has to adjust his composition in fluent forms to the needs of a fairly definite dramatic story; but the difficulty does not release an artist from the responsibility of aiming at the ideal.

The outlook is not so discouraging after all; for it is a fact that the artist is emancipated, rather than restricted, by the conditions of organizing motion into totality. First, he may run the whole range from absolute rest or lack of motion, through slow movement, to movement of the utmost speed. He may present these motion values simultaneously or in any succession. His subject may, for example, be a rock-bound coast in the background, a ship sailing majestic-ally over the gentle ground swell of the sea, and a hydro-aëroplane swooping down in the foreground; or at some other time it may be the gradual acceleration of motion when a seemingly phlegmatic and imperturb-able mob is roused to acts of ungovernable fury. Sec-ond, his movements may be of any scope, from the eruption of a volcano to the winking of an owlet's eye. Third, the movement may be in any direction with reference to the observer. It may be directly or diagonally toward or away from him. It may be across his field of vision from either side, from the top or from the bottom. Fourth, the observer in the theatre may take the place of the camera and follow the moving object, thus getting, for example, the ef-fect of landscape rushing by a train window, or of the earth sliding back beneath an aëroplane. Fifth, by the device of double exposure one picture may be dissolved into the next, as one note may blend into another in music. The musician who orchestrates a piece of music for a whole orchestra does not have more latitude than the cinema composer.

One difference between musical composition and cinematic composition must be kept in mind; it is that in a motion picture there are no rests, no absences of pictures to correspond to the silences between musical notes. On the screen the edges of pictorial values cannot well be separated; they must touch as closely as the negatives in the film. This makes it all the more important to be careful of the joining. If pictures are not properly joined they will break in the aesthetic test just as surely as in the projecting machine.

To begin with, a composition in fluent forms must have unity, otherwise it cannot be called a single composition, if a composition at all. We have all seen photoplays that possessed about as much unity as a bead string made of diamonds, rubies, shoe buttons, pearls, perforated pennies, bits of glass, wampum beads, and gold nuggets, or as a succession of the following sounds in the order named: a whistle, a piano note, a voice, a drum, a flute note, an organ note, the bark of a dog, the tolling of a bell, and the note of a fife. The memory of any one of these sounds clashes with our perception of the next. And no given sound leads us to expect the next one. Such arrangement of parts do not comprise a totality and cannot leave a single great impression on the mind. The Fox photoplay *The Daughter of the Gods* is a conspicuous violation of the principle of unity. The good fairies and bad witches of Northern lore roam familiarly in Oriental harems or along African coasts; mermaids dwell with Santa Clauses or dwarfs; these dwarfs are in turn transformed into Men of Valour, or Hosts of the Cross, which are obviously reminiscent of Joan of Arc; the poetic theme of the transmigration of souls clashes with a veritable Noah's Ark or menagerie of the following animals: cats, toads, donkeys, oxen, camels, pigs, sheep, dogs, horses, and crocodiles, fraternizing with blue birds, song birds, pigeons, peacocks, gulls, and swans. A beautiful Arab encampment is forgotten when we come to the wild surf of a sea which is supposed to be notoriously calm, and this in turn is obliterated by the spectacular scenes of a burning city. Such a jumble, besides being incoherent and meaningless to the mind, has no unity of visual impression for the eye.

In a melody the notes must be in the same key and even of the same instrument; in a cinematic composition the pictures, though of various subjects, should be in the same visual key. Now swans and pigeons may be in the same key, but crocodiles and sheep are not. Mermaids and harem beauties may be in the same key, but mermaids and camels are not. The lines, tones, and textures of pigeons and swans or of harem beauties and mermaids harmonize with each other; but the lines, tones, and textures of crocodiles and sheep or of mermaids and camels do not harmonize with each other. And the lack of harmony is apparent even when these subjects are exhibited several minutes apart on the screen.

The Daughter of the Gods lacks both unity of story and unity of visual appeals; but it would be almost as bad artistically even if it had the former and did not have the latter. Imagine how Dvorak's "Humoresque" would sound if the first few notes were played on a violin, the next few on a slide trombone, the next on a piano, the next on an ukelele, the next on a pipe organ, the next on a cornet, the next on a violoncello, etc., to the end of the piece. Such a performance might present proper continuity, might present the notes of the music in their original tempo and pitch, might, therefore, be said to have a certain unity of content, and yet it would be an utter farce because it lacked all unity of expression. But miscellaneous and chaotic appeals to the ear are no worse than miscellaneous and chaotic appeals to the eye. A photoplay cannot make a single abiding impression on the beholder unless it has its entire succession of subjects, of lines, shapes, tones, colours, organized into a unity.

But a fluent unity, like a static unity, must have emphasis somewhere. Just as in a story some characters and some events must have greater significance than others, so in a succession of pictures some must have greater eye appeal than others. And the need of emphasis is by no means incompatible with the need of unity. In fact, unity implies emphasis because it involves subordination as well as co-ordination of its parts. One method of securing emphasis in a photoplay is to increase the tempo of the pictures as the story approaches a climax. This is admirably illustrated in Griffith's *Intolerance*. He has managed to bring the climaxes of his four interwoven stories close together. And as the photoplay approaches this group of climaxes the action within the scenes is accelerated and the scenes themselves are gradually shortened until they become mere flashes, all this producing a staccato effect which almost overwhelms the eye with its power.

Another type of dramatic emphasis may be secured on occasion by decreasing the tempo, that is, by retarding the action within the scenes, and lengthening the scenes themselves, thus gradually producing the effect of solemnity and majesty of action.

The pitch of pictures, that is, the sharpness of values may also be altered to produce emphasis. A scene, beginning in the low pitch of light greys and dark greys may gradually heighten into the strong sharpness of steel whites and ebony blacks; and then, after the moment of emphasis has passed, may again subside into a low pitch.

Emphasis may also be produced by arrangement of tonal values wherever the subject permits. For example, the eye gives particular attention to, and the spectator is sure to remember a single moonlight scene in·blue if it appears isolated among a succession of scenes representing the yellowish light of day.

The composer of fluent forms must constantly beware lest his composition become merely a succession of vanishing aspects. Painters, who deal with static forms, often manage to suggest motion; yet in every case a painting is really an arrested moment of repose, and its impressiveness to the beholder is due partly to the fact that he may devote any length of time to the contemplation of the chosen moment of repose. But in a photoplay the values vanish while we look upon them. A similar vanishing of values occurs in music. Yet they may not vanish forever, because the composer has arranged a rhythmic recurrence of certain fundamental notes or motifs. In a Wagner opera, for example, the recurring note or motif gradually impresses itself upon our minds until we remember it exactly and feel its full significance. The musician therefore with all his fluent, ever vanishing forms succeeds in creating a static effect, a base of rest to which the hearer's attention may return again and again for contemplation. Thus in the photoplay a beautiful subject, a beautiful static composition which has appeared on the screen for only a few minutes may be recalled again and again at rhythmic intervals during the play until its full beauty is impressed upon the eye and mind of the beholder.

This emphasis by repetition is to be recommended only, of course, when the picture or pictorial value repeated is really worthy of emphasis. The figure, grouping, object, landscape, or whatever pictorial value repeated must have something more than mere surface value, something that cannot be fully appreciated by hasty inspection, a visual beauty and dramatic significance that grows by repetition. Just as a motif in music or a refrain in poetry takes on a new beauty with each new context in which it is presented, so a repeated picture in a photoplay should gain new meaning and beauty each time it is recalled in a succession of new pictures. An interesting case of the recurring note is furnished by *Intolerance*. The scene of a young woman rocking a baby in a crude cradle, accompanied by a sub-title from Walt Whitman, " Out of the cradle endlessly rocking," was repeated scores (it seemed hundreds) of times. Just what the picture symbolized was not clear to all of the beholders of the photoplay, but those to whom it did symbolize something were greatly impressed by the cogency of this constantly recurring note. In *Intolerance* it might have been, or in some other photoplay it may be, artistically effective to repeat with variation. In *Intolerance*, for example, the general motif might have been the mother putting her child to sleep, but the aspect of the cradle and the domestic surroundings might have varied with the countries and periods of history represented in the play. In any case emphasis may result from the recurring picture, which, once familiar to the eye, gradually becomes fixed in the mind.

Further, emphasis may be secured by the contrast of fluent forms. We all know the effect of contrast when values are shown simultaneously. If a tall man and a short man appear on the stage together the tall man looks taller than he really is and the short man looks shorter than he really is. The same effect may be obtained when values are shown successively. A flood of red on the screen will seem all the more red if it is preceded by a flood of green. These things are due to optical laws and not to the sentiments, tastes, or experience of the individual beholder. The vertical lines of tall slender spruce trees will gain in emphasis when contrasted with the long horizontal lines of the sea. The effects of contrast need not, of course, be confined to the realm of colours and lines. A palace may be contrasted with a hovel, or a lady with a strumpet. Whatever the contrast is it must be a contrast in kind, that is, a difference between similar values. For example, a cat may be in contrast with a tiger, but could not be said to be in contrast with an iceberg. The latter is a clash, not a contrast.

Now if the whole succession of ever originating, ever vanishing values in a photoplay has unity and emphasis, it will be still more pleasing if it also embodies the principle of balance. In the previous chapter we have explained what is meant by balance of subject, line, and tone in a painting, that is, in a composition in static forms. It is obvious that fluent forms, too, must be in balance. It is not enough that the end of a cinema plot as such be in balance with the beginning of that plot; it is important that the visual values at the end of a motion picture be in balance with the values at the beginning of that picture.   Again we find an analogy in music.   The last note returns to the first, an equilibrium is struck, and the ear is pleased.   But balance applies even further than beginnings and ends.   Continuous balance at all times is desirable.   So in a succession of a dozen or more pictures some of those pictures should balance others in line or tone or general pattern.   At some "movie" theatre you see a run of pictures something like this: a peasant girl herding sheep; a close-up of her face, emphasizing her eyebrows; a close-up of her dog attacked by a rattlesnake; a company of archers and lancers storming an old grey tower; and a young fisherman at sea hauling in his nets.   This does not look especially promising, and yet, if we omit the eyebrows and rattlesnake as unnecessary interpolations, we may find considerable visual balance between the soft grey tones of the sheep and the tower, between the sharp lines of the ship's rigging and the bows and lances, even between the bright gleam of the fish and the lance heads.   Now, providing the fisherman, the peasant girl, and one of the archers are woven into a story, this may turn out to be a fairly artistic progression of pictures after all.

Balance may be applied to the tempo, as well as to the subject matter, tones, and lines of a cinematic composition.   Just as in music quarter notes, half notes, and whole notes are proportionally distributed, so in a photoplay there should be a general balance of pictorial durations.   There would certainly be a feeling of unstable equilibrium at seeing a photoplay in which the pictures of the first two reels were all fifteen seconds or less in length and the pictures of the remaining reels were all two minutes or more in length.

A photoplay which is characterized by unity, emphasis, and balance will be all the more beautiful as a creation of art if it possesses the quality of rhythm. In the previous chapter we have tried to explain what is meant by rhythm in the pictorial lines and tones which are grasped simultaneously by the eye. A little reflection will convince any one that rhythm may, or may not, characterize the pictorial values which the eye perceives successively, just as it may, or may not, characterize the auditory values which the ear perceives successively in music. We have pointed out that rhythm consists, not in mathematical repetition, but in repetition with variation. In a composition of fluent forms rhythm must, of course, be progressive, proceeding from the past, through the present, into the future. In a cinematic composition, therefore, the pictorial values which are immediately present to the eye should form a rhythmical progression from the values which have just passed, toward those which are about to come.

Suppose we take three beautiful or interesting pictures of a mansion, a factory, and a brook respectively, each picture a half minute in length. Suppose we arrange them in this order: mansion-factory-brook-mansion - factory - brook - mansion - factory - brook, etc. The effect would certainly not be rhythmical. Or suppose we take the three musical notes C, E, and G and arrange them all as quarter notes in the following order: C-E-G-C-E-G-C-E-G, etc. The effect would certainly not be rhythmical. But these three notes arranged in various pitches and lengths constitute the hundred or more bugle calls used by the United States Army and Navy. Now there is, of course, not one chance in a million that a photoplay director should arrange his pictures in mathematically accurate repetitions. But there are several hundred thousand chances in a million that his succession of pictures will be without any semblance of system whatsoever. He certainly cannot trust to accident for an orderly arrangement, any more than the musician can write the names of his notes on slips of paper, shake them up in a hat, and trust to accident for his melody.

Pictures, we have said, like musical notes, possess tone, pitch, stress, duration, and rate of repetition. The interweaving of these values in a beautiful rhythm must be the product of genius and not of calculation. And when this subtle thing, rhythm, has been produced, its effect on the spectator will be inevitable, even though he may never understand or be able to explain just what it was that made the run of pictures so pleasing to the eye.

The cinema composer must remember that in trying to achieve unity, emphasis, balance, and rhythm in the composition of fluent visible forms he will meet with all of the hardships and discouragements of the pioneer. The hard-headed money maker will tell him to leave all such finical tinkerings to old maids or people who write books about the art of the motion picture. The " star " will insist that he or she be given at least three close-ups in every reel, as though the pictorial value of a photoplay were guaranteed only when the spectator could distinguish the eyelashes or count the molars of the " star." The publicity man will demand that the villain be lashed to a torpedo and fired into a dynamite ship, or be disposed of in some other " picturesque " way. But the pioneer will run the gauntlet of injunctions, jeers, and threats, will steadfastly follow the gleam of art, for he may be confident that the world which has appreciated and paid for the best in sculpture, architecture, painting, poetry, drama, and music will some day appreciate and pay for the best in the new art of cinema composition. Each of the elder arts has some unique characteristic, some function which it alone among the arts can perform. The distinctive rôle of the motion picture play is to give refined pleasure to a cultured world by mobilizing the ever originating, ever vanishing visible forms which nature can produce or imagination can transform into the material of art.

But the cinema composer may not succeed in perfecting the composition of fluent visual values in a given play, or, if he does succeed, he may find that the play is still not a wholly satisfactory piece of work. We must therefore proceed to the consideration of other ways and means of making a photoplay impressive to an audience.

CHAPTER V

For thousands of years the public, old and young alike, have gazed spell-bound at exhibitions of the marvellous, things which were remote from ordinary human experience or by the illusion of magic completely transcended natural powers. This primitive enjoyment of the wonderful is perennial. Today the fastest runner, the most agile jumper, the man with the highest batting average, the most spectacular aviator, has as many open-mouthed ejaculating admirers as did the gladiator in the days of imperial Rome. And the Hindoo magician who disappears up a rope ladder into the sky evokes as much astonishment as the sorcerers of Pharaoh who turned rods into serpents. The ancient world craved something even more amazing than the exhibitions of athletes, acrobats, and magicians; it desired to be thrilled by things which surpassed even the powers of these exceptional performers. Therefore men of inventive genius fabricated stories of the supernatural, of gods and devils, of giants and elves, of witches and trolls, with their astounding catalog of powers and achievements. Of course, neither these remarkable beings nor their gifts could be perceived by human eyes, for they existed only in the imaginations of those who told the stories and those who heard them.

Before going farther in this discussion let us differentiate between the sense of wonder or marvel and the play of imagination. Man marvels at things which he actually perceives to be, or believes to be, real, real and supernormal. Thus he marvels at Niagara Falls, or the Woolworth Tower, or the supreme gifts of some remarkable man. At such things he experiences a sense of wonder which amounts practically to a physical sensation, for his eyes open wide, his lips part, and his breast heaves. On the other hand, if he thought that these things were merely figments of the imagination, his feeling of wonder or amazement would not exist; yet his mind would dwell pleasantly on the fiction, for man naturally enjoys the indulgence of fancy. It is a pleasant pastime of the mind to imagine castles in the air, or giants twenty feet tall, or spirits walking in the night, or fairies dwelling in the calyx of a lily. But such supernatural things, while they please our fancy, do not make us marvel, unless we believe that they actually exist.

· Now we of today were not content merely to imagine the phenomena of epic poetry, of religious tradition, of myths, of fairyland; we had to invent a machine which would materialize these fancies and bring them before our very eyes. The cinematograph is the great magician of the twentieth century which permits us to see with our physical eyes the things which our forebears since the world began saw only in their imagination.

The motion picture itself is a scientific achievement which to many theatre-goers still seems little short of magic. One marvels not only at the fact that the picture on the screen moves but that it reproduces faithfully and accurately the motions that have taken place weeks, months, or years ago. Suppose it were possible this very evening to go and see authentic films of events that took place hundreds of years ago, of Columbus setting sail in his three ships, of Shakespeare acting in his own plays, of Napoleon going into battle. How we would marvel at such a visual restoration of the past! But we cannot see the actual cinema records of these motions; we can only imagine them. You imagined them more or less vividly just now as you read these words. Who knows? Perhaps it is pleasanter to imagine the deeds of the past than to see them in their actuality. At any rate, in this and the following chapter we must distinguish between the appeal to the sense of wonder and the appeal to the imagination. And, whether in any particular case it is an advantage or a disadvantage, it is certain that the cinematograph may present to our eyes, to our sense of wonder, many things which formerly were presented only to our imagination.

One of the most common examples of camera magic is the metamorphosis, or transformation, a phenomenon which myths and fairy tales have long led us to imagine, but which we may now actually see on the screen. Transformations of statues into human beings, flowers into fairies, waterfalls into giants, and old hags into trees are familiar to every devotee of the motion pictures. These things are mysterious, but they are no longer imaginary; you see them, and I see them on the screen; they are real, if we are to believe the testimony of our own eyes. Perhaps even the child at the theatre does not really believe that the statue is a real statue, or that it really turns into a human being; nevertheless that child marvels at the

magical thing he sees, just as surely as any adult
marvels at the inexplicable trick of the magician on
the stage. This new appeal, the appeal to the sense
of wonder, is a thing which the scenario writer and the
photoplay director may conjure with. If they turn
the trick badly they will only disgust, or at best, amuse
the spectators with their awkwardness; but if they
have genius for plot making and mechanical execu-
tion, they may, for a few moments at least, cast a
spell of wonder over those who come to see the motion pictures.

Thus the camera may materialize the startling
metamorphoses of myth makers. It may also actualize such hallucinations as ghosts and visions, illusions
of real life, illusions, however, which many people
even today look upon as realities. Ghosts have, of
course, been presented in stage plays from the beginning of drama, but never with the convincingness now
possible in the photoplay. Banquo's ghost in the original performance of *Macbeth* was undoubtedly acted
by the same actor who had a few minutes before acted
the part of the living Banquo. The ghost was just
as real, just as heavy, and perspired just as much as
Banquo, and differed from him only in having " gory
locks." Modern developments in stage mechanics and
stage craft have enabled producers of *Macbeth, Hamlet,* and *Richard III* to represent the ghosts with more
spiritistic, more supernatural effect. But no stage
production has ever yet succeeded in presenting the
airiness, the marvellous elusiveness, the delicate fading
from invisibility into visibility and back again which
is possible in the motion pictures. Further, these effects of double exposure permit many subtle renderings

which are denied to the stage performance. For example, Macbeth may see the ghost in his own chair; he cries out and turns away in horror, but when the astonished lords look at the designated place the ghost has faded out into nothingness. Such literal interpretation of what Shakespeare's text leads us to imagine is possible only on the motion picture screen. There is a gain in verisimilitude and convincingness, too, in the fact that the photoplay ghost may be presented in broad daylight. The spectator cannot say to himself that the ghost is only an illusion of the night and will vanish when light comes, for there on the screen he sees the ghost, faintly but surely, and any other spectator will corroborate the testimony of his eyes.

Closely allied to the illusion of ghosts is the illusion of visions. In history and in story books we read of the visions seen by real and imaginary characters, and we merely imagine the visions seen. But in the photoplay we, too, may see the visions, and may feel more clearly the emotions experienced by the characters affected. Thus in the photoplay *Joan, the Woman* we may feel with the heroine a thrilling inspiration as she sees a mounted knight in full armour and panoply riding in the air above the assembled multitude. She is transfixed by the vision, but when the people about her look upward at the object of her gaze they see nothing but empty air. We in the audience marvel as we see the mysterious knight, very faintly but definitely enough to be sure that he is there, and in a moment, quicker than words, we grasp the thoughts of Joan, and the comments of the crowd upon her supposed madness. This is camera magic, a dramatic effect, which can, of course, never be rivalled in a similar performance on the legitimate stage.

Through camera magic the sizes and shapes of people, animals, and things may depart from the actual to the fantastical. Millions of readers have enjoyed imagining the fantastic conceptions in *Gulliver's Travels,* but now for the first time we may see an actual motion photograph of a twenty-four foot Gulliver holding a six-inch Lilliputian in the hollow of his hand. Perhaps we had not imagined a Gulliver with exactly those features, or a Lilliputian with exactly that costume, but there, nevertheless, before our eyes is the impossible reality. All of us except the infant may know that the strange effect is due to a trick of double exposure, yet we and the infant alike are open-eyed with wonder at the exhibition. By the same trick animals may be represented as fabulously large. For example, in the Lasky film adaptation of Stevenson's *The Bottle Imp* two real lions guarding the doorway to a palace seem as large as elephants in comparison with the men who are entering that doorway. Any one of us may go to the menagerie and see real lions, but only in the photoplay may we marvel at real lions as large as elephants.

Skilful directors may achieve fantastic sizes and shapes even without resorting to double exposure. For example, in the Artcraft version of *The Poor Little Rich Girl* the actress, Mary Pickford, was made to seem very tiny by contrast with the abnormally large things surrounding her. The door knob was so high that she could hardly reach it, chairs were so high that she could hardly climb up on them, the steps leading up to the Stock Exchange were so enormous that she climbed from one to another with great difficulty. All these contrasts produced the desired effect because it is somehow easier and more natural for the audience to think of a baby girl than of gigantic doors, chairs, and steps. A still more shrewd method was used in the *Daughter of the Gods*. It was based on the psychological law that whenever we are shown the picture of any isolated thing, with no other relative thing to establish its size, we think of that thing as normal in size. Thus when we were shown the picture of a tree we subconsciously judged it to be a tree of normal size, perhaps two feet or possibly three feet in diameter. With that norm established in our minds we would naturally infer the relative size of anything new that came into the picture. Now the tree was as a matter of fact some twelve feet in diameter; therefore when Anitia (Annette Kellermann) appeared beside the tree, our illusion as to size made her seem diminutive by comparison. Then the illusion as to her size being kept up, we judged the dwarfs (played by children) to be extremely diminutive. In other words, Anitia, a full grown woman, seemed a mere child, which made the dwarfs, really children, seem like mere dolls.

The cinema composer who undertakes to cinematize fairyland must always remember that he is robbing imagination by supplying something real instead of the imagined, and that he cannot be successful in the substitution unless he presents something not only real, but really amazing, something that appeals to the sense of wonder. To be thus successful he must be a wizard himself; his tricks must be based on the psychology of illusion as firmly as the tricks of the stage magician. The conjuror cannot please his audience unless he successfully deceives them; so the cinema conjuror must catch the spectators' minds off guard and lead them captive into the realm of wonder.

In cinema land even the laws of nature may be reversed or set aside. A brook may be shown flowing merrily up hill; people may be shown sitting down to dinner with their feet on the ceilings, partaking of their soup quite unaware of the fact that they are living upside down; a man may jump to the top of a high tower, or he may be flattened thin as paper by a steam roller only to rise again into erect plumpness and saunter away; an apple blossom may mature into a ripe apple within a few minutes, and while you are rubbing your eyes the apple may diminish into a blossom, and the blossom into a bud; castles may stand majestically in mid air; the squirrel may carry a forest on his back; the mountain may crack a nut, and the tail may wag the dog. It would be possible by exposing a film slowly through a period of twenty years to show a man growing in five minutes from babyhood to manhood. In cinema land fairy stories may come true, because not even the laws of nature herself can confine the rare sorcery of the camera.

The cinema composer may even breathe the spirit of life and personality into inanimate objects. A familiar example of such conjuring is the animated letters and words that assemble into their places in some advertisement on the screen. They run, jump, fly, and roll into their appointed places, some latecomer crowding the others apart, the " i " almost losing her dot in the shuffle, and the " Q " getting his tail stepped on by the broad footed " A." It often happens in everyday life that an object acts as though it had a cantankerous personality. Any golf player, any owner of a cheap motor car, any one who has ever handled tools, any boy who has ever made a kite can testify that dead objects may act as if they were alive and possessed of devils. On the screen such strange suspicions can be verified. For example, in *The Bottle Imp* the bottle itself is certainly a live specimen of tantalizing mischief. It jumps away from the owner when he grasps after it; it bounces against his head when he is not looking, all this because the imp is really in it. Animated objects of pleasanter personalities may be seen in other plays. Perhaps a brave, noble pair of boots goes calling on a coy little pair of slippers, takes them out walking, and bids them lovingly good-by; or perhaps a set of A B C blocks build themselves into a magnificent house, all without help of visible hands, while their pretty little owner lies sound asleep.

Enough has been said to illustrate the wonder-working magic of the camera. Any writer who has a genius for the whimsical would do well to consider the effectiveness of telling his story in motion pictures instead of in words. And any cinema composer who wishes to master all the means of pleasing the eyes and impressing the minds of his audience must learn to wield the wand of camera magic. This appeal to the sense of wonder is one of the unique possibilities of the motion picture play. And it must be remembered that any art reaches its highest achievement through those functions in which it surpasses the other arts. Neither painting nor sculpture, neither dance nor drama, nor even magician of the stage can work the pleasantly uncanny and delightfully impossible miracles of the screen. This is one of the fields of cinema composition which should be exploited by creative minds until it has developed from the stage of trickery and mere cleverness to the stage of enthralling art. And, in every case, the element of camera magic, however large or small it may be, must be properly fused with the element of the pictorial and the element of the dramatic.

Now it may occur to some reflecting person that the photoplay, because it can actualize so many things formerly left to the imagination of the reader, is a hard matter-of-fact thing which leaves no opportunity for the individual spectator's deviation of fancy. Such a notion is entirely wrong. We shall show in the following chapter that the photoplay, despite its weird actualities, may still in many new ways appeal to the imagination of the spectator.

CHAPTER VI

THE APPEAL TO THE IMAGINATION

THE ideal photoplay pleases the eye of the spectator, it appeals to his sense of wonder, it stirs and quiets his emotions, and mildly taxes his judgment; but it would cease to be ideal if it did not also pleasantly stimulate his imagination. No art is perfect unless it makes such an appeal. When we stand before a beautiful painting, an impressive piece of sculpture, or a magnificent cathedral, our fancy soars far beyond the physical things upon which our eyes are resting. When we listen to good music our imagination is constantly at work painting shadowy and fleeting pictures. When we read an appealing book our mind leaps from the printed words into a dream-realm of our own making. If the photoplay is to develop the power of a genuine art it, too, must be full of suggestion; it must appeal to the mind's eye as well as to the body's eye.

But the pride of the photographers, of the directors, and even of many theorists who have written books about the photoplay, is that the cinema leaves nothing to the imagination. That these men should develop such a mistaken enthusiasm is but natural, because the motion picture has the amazing power of capturing physically and projecting on the screen a vast number of things which in the stage play had to be left entirely to the imagination. The mere mechanician is tempted to photograph or " fake " everything, from tiny animals on the bottom of the sea to the molten struggles in the crater of Vesuvius, from the burial of a fairy on a rose petal to the departing soul of a man. It would impress all of us deeply to discover that a man's soul could actually be photographed, but we would be impressed by a scientific achievement and not by an artistic expression. It must be remembered that, while science and machinery starve the imagination, art sets it free.

The secret of human enjoyment in imagining things is that every individual can imagine what he pleases, independent of everybody else in the world. Every one, from the toddling infant to the venerable grandfather, thus creates his own kingdom, which no war, or tempest, or fire, or flood can harm. Nobody wants to be deprived of this individuality, this very ownness of his fancy world. Let us contrast the uniformity of actual fact with the million deviations of fancy. This capital letter " A " appears exactly the same to every one who looks upon it, and to every one who sees other impressions from the same font of type and on the same stock of paper. You cannot *imagine* this " A," because you *see* it. Nor can you *imagine* the letter which was upon your childhood blocks, because you *remember* that; and every one who paid any close attention to those blocks remembers the same letter. But you can and must imagine the scarlet letter " A " which the unfortunate Hester Prynne embroidered upon her dress, because you have never seen that letter and you never can see it in exact and concrete form. No two people who have read or heard of Hawthorne's novel could ever agree in imagining exactly the same size, shape, materials, and position of that letter.

This appeal to the individual's own imagination is one of the qualities of every literary masterpiece. Almost any line taken at random from Shakespeare will illustrate. In the tragedy of *Hamlet* Horatio and Marcellus, watching through the night, have seen the ghost and are still talking about the fearful apparition, when Horatio perceives the dawn and alludes to it in the following lines:

> "But look! The morn in russet mantle clad
> Walks o'er the dew of yon high eastern hill."

What a manifold appeal these lines contain! We may imagine the appearance of the two actors on the Shakespearean stage, more than three hundred years ago. Or we imagine the dawn which they pretended to see. Or we try to realize the figure of speech,—morn like a human being, or a god perhaps, robed in a russet mantle, stately and solemn, walking toward us over a dewy hilltop. Or we wonder what the actors imagined as they spoke those lines, or what Shakespeare imagined as he wrote them. There is no end to the play of our fancies. You and I read the same seventeen words. But the pictures we imagine, though similar, are as different as the clouds of an autumn sky.

Now let us suppose that the poetic figure of the dawn had been presented to us, not in verse, but through the medium of a painting, or of a photograph. Then we should all have seen the same figure, the same shape, bearing and stride, the same mantle, the same hill and sky; and forever we would remember, not imagine, the morn in russet mantle clad. Here is the inferiority and dull commonness of many a motion picture; it makes the spectator a slave to the screen because it forces him to receive mentally only those things which everybody else perceives at the same moment and in exactly the same details. It should not be so, and it is not necessary. In the photoplay we must always have pictures, of course. But beyond, and about these physical pictures, may be the fancy-filled regions of empty air.

To begin with, a photoplay tableau can always be so arranged that part of it is " off stage." In Mr. De Mille's *Carmen* the opening picture is a high rocky coast with the sea beating in. On a rock in the foreground stands a gipsy with his back towards us, looking off to the sea and waving at some one. What is on that sea? Ocean liners or yachts with silver sails? To whom is he waving? A comrade? A rescuing party? A band of smugglers? We in the audience cannot see, and therefore we may imagine, each in his own individual way. The picture on the screen is within the frame, but within it in such a way that our fancy leaps beyond the frame. This device of suggesting objects and actions outside the frame of the screen picture is an inheritance from the stage drama, which made a virtue of necessity and suggested things " off stage " which it could not convincingly bring before the eyes of an audience. Thus the naval battle in Shakespeare's *Anthony and Cleopatra* or the burning of the orphanage in Ibsen's *Ghosts* must be reported by messengers and may be vividly realized by the audience through the effect upon the characters on the stage. The very fact that the motion pictures can represent these spectacular actions so well is a danger to the photoplaywright. He must constantly beware lest he crowd his canvas with bulky facts that overburden memory and clog the imagination. Let him rather suggest part of his picture by leaving it outside of the frame.

Or let the scenario writer utilize the vague and subtle effect of distance, the far away backgrounds of nature herself. This effect of natural perspective the playwright of the stage cannot produce, because the distance from the foreground to the background on the ordinary theatre stage is never more than fifty or sixty feet. But the cinema photographer is limited only by the horizon of the great out of doors. And he must remember that moving figures, indistinct in the distance, always stimulate the observer's fancy. It is a law of the cultivated mind that it resents things that are made too obvious, too clear. Thus we say that a joke is spoiled when it is explained. We take pride in being able to get the point without any explanation. So, too, in a representation to the eye we enjoy completing the picture for ourselves, even though some of the details are dim or missing. This law is observed in drawing and painting. Glance at any line drawing, a cartoon, for example, and you will see that the lines are broken and incomplete; yet your eye unconsciously bridges these gaps. Look at Monet's "Cathedral at Rouen" and you see the front of the cathedral heavily veiled in a greyish blue atmosphere. The painting has no detail, no sharpness; yet behind that atmosphere your imagination follows the delicate traceries in carven stone. Stand before the ruins of a mediaeval castle and soon you will imagine that castle in splendid perfection, surrounded by knights in armour and ringing with the revelry of the banquet hall.

"The motion picture can borrow and can even heighten some of these effects, because to the dim figures in the distance it can add movement, movement of a mysterious slowness." And, by the way, this slow movement of figures in the background often comes as a pleasant relief to the hysterically rapid movements in the foreground. Such quiet and mysterious intervals we occasionally see in some raw and violent western melodrama which is still being cranked out to the five cent public. In the foreground the ranchmen and cowboys are busily branding cattle; while on the brow of the distant hill five or six Indian scouts are prowling about, rising from the rocks one moment and the next disappearing into the shadows. In D'Annunzio's *Cabiria* comes a peculiarly satisfying scene where we look off to a caravan moving slowly, distant and indistinct, over the desert, the dark figures of men and camels standing out against the soft yellow of the sands. A different but allied effect is produced in the film version of Service's *The Shooting of Dan McGrew* where a slender dog train fights its way over the sharp whiteness of a snowy waste in Alaska. In the Blue Bird photoplay *Undine* we get the right atmosphere of mythology and fairy lore when we see the graceful white forms of sea nymphs disporting in the surf and on the sloping banks across the bay. In all these pictures the magic of distance throws the spectator into a momentary reverie, when his imagination weaves beauties which would depreciate or disappear if brought close to the searching lens of the camera.

Another pleasing effect which the motion picture camera can easily achieve is the "representation of figures in silhouette." The eye is rested and pleased by the uniform dark tone of the figure, and the fancy is set to work because, despite sharpness of outline, the content and texture of the figure is neutral and uninforming.   One may experience a peculiarly poetic feeling from seeing a humble country church dark against the afterglow of a Kansas sunset; one may feel the same mood when seeing the history-haunted cathedral of Notre Dame de Paris standing inscrutable and primitive as a mountain against the silver sky of a full moon.   Even more appealing is the silhouette of a human figure in motion.   Hiawatha at the close of his last day steps into his birch canoe and paddles slowly up the fiery path of the setting sun, his gaunt, dark body growing smaller with the distance until it mingles with the radiance of eternity.   Even when the movement is slight the effect is appealing.   Our melancholy heroine leaves her sleepless bed and sits at the window looking off into the moonlight, her noble profile sombre against the luminous sky.[1]   In *Undine* one of the silhouette pictures is a perfect three tone pictorial composition.   Some girls come down of a late afternoon to bathe in the sun-washed sea.   Before disrobing they pause for a moment in graceful pose; their bodies are in deep shadow, and a soft half tone is in the sunlight intercepted by their transparent draperies, all contrasting with the high light in the steel whiteness of the sea.   The absence of detail in all these pictures stimulates our fancies, and lifts us into the realm of the ideal.   Crude realities cannot

[1] See page 96.

From the *Lady Carew*. A good example of ... ... in landscape. ... ... how ever, would ... ... shown going instead of coming. See Chapters III and VIII

From *Sweet Kitty Bellairs*. The spectator enjoys a silhouette picture because it rests the eye and gives the imagination a chance to supply the omitted or suppressed details. See page 96.

offend because they are not there, and our imagination always paints things more beautiful than they are.

A pictorial effect allied to that of the silhouette is the shadow of a figure or of an object which we cannot see. There is something poetic and mysterious in this unsubstantial evidence of things not seen. In the last chapter of Anatole France's *Le Livre de Mon Ami* the narrator tells of an extraordinary incident which occurred one night while he was stopping at a country inn. He was sitting before the fireplace waiting for the supper which his hostess, a hag-like creature, was preparing, when he suddenly observed on the opposite wall the immobile shadow of a beautiful young girl. He was charmed by the lovely profile and figure, but when he turned to look for the girl herself he was astonished to find no other person in the room except the busy hostess. When he had assured himself that no girl was in the house or had been there that evening, he was informed by the hostess that years ago other men of his family had seen the same shadow on the same wall and that the haunting apparition must be a punishment of God. The young man was mystified and was left to wonder during the rest of his life whether he had seen a hereditary ghost or had inherited the gift of dreams.

The modern theatre is well equipped for the fanciful suggestion of physical causes by the representation of physical effects alone. An excellent example is the charming fairy Tinker Bell in Barrie's *Peter Pan,* a sprite whom the audience can never realize in the flesh, for she exists only as a patch of light flitting about the stage, fading into pathetic dimness when death is near and glowing into joyful radiance only when the audience saves her life by declaring their belief in fairies.

❝ Such imaginative effects in the theatre can be rivalled or surpassed through the magic of the camera or the wizardry of the motion picture studio if the director is himself endowed with imagination. ❞ When we look about for examples in the photoplays produced up to date we discover that shadow effects, though often occurring with certain pictorial values, are usually not remote from their substantial cause and therefore lose their appeal of mystery. The shadow of a pretty bathing girl parading over the beach has no very strong appeal if the girl herself is before our eyes. In the Blue Bird photoplay *The Secret of the Swamp* the old major believes that he has shot his neighbour, the deacon, and fears that the deacon has crawled off to the swamp to die. On the next day the remorseful major is peering off towards the swamp and is horrified to see some buzzards circling overhead as if they had discovered carrion. He sickens at the thought and is crossing his lawn for the refuge of his own chamber when he is intensely shocked by a buzzard's shadow crossing his path. Here the effect of distance at first and shadow afterwards might have had some appeal if the director had not fettered our fancy by interpolating realistic close-ups of the buzzards alighting on a fence. In Ince's consistently crude spectacle *Civilization* there is one little poetical and refreshing touch in the pictures of the mobilization. When the masses of troops are marching heavily across the city plaza we suddenly see the shadows of three aeroplanes sliding silently and with trackless course over the street and houses and troops, and our imaginations immediately soar to the clouds and begin weaving the destinies of the venturesome bird-men. And the poetic value still remains even after we have been informed by the publicity man that the aviators were not in the employ of the producer and that the effect of the shadows was the result merely of a strange coincidence.

The cinema composer must not infer from our enthusiastic championing of subtle and imaginative effects that we would have a photoplay all "off screen," or dim in the distances, or in silhouettes and shadows. Too much seasoning spoils any soup, and diamonds would not be worth stealing if they were as common as dew drops. If the Bray-Gilbert silhouette cartoons are not destined to become classic photo-plays it is because they are all shadow, all silhouette, and by this limited means of expression tire the eye and cloy the imagination.

We have been discussing visual images in the mind of the spectator, but there is such a thing also as auditory imagination, and the very silence of the screen drama may sometimes be enlisted in the service of art. Keats in his *Ode on a Grecian Urn* has achieved the strange effect of making movement eternal because it is static, and melodies sweet because they are unheard. By merely looking at the simple decorations on the side of the urn the poet could imagine the ecstatic sounds of pipes and timbrels, and the passionate utterance of the lover pursuing for-ever his forever fleeing maiden. A good example of auditory imagination may be found in Griffith's film version of Browning's *Pippa Passes*. Pippa, the silk winder, on her one day of vacation strolls through the village playing her guitar and singing a song with the refrain

"God's in His Heaven
All's right with the world."

The words and musical score have been thrown on the screen, and as we watch the girl we hear in fancy her voice and the accompaniment of the guitar. Her singing has a salutary effect on the inmates of more than one house where crime is being hatched. The criminals suddenly pause in their plotting and assume the attitude of listening. Their expressions change to rapt attention. We in the audience can easily imagine the song they hear and the figure of the singer passing by. To us the very silence is strangely musical. If some stupid exhibitor wishes to rob the play of this subtle appeal let him hire some soprano of village fame to step before the screen and warble out the notes of Pippa's magic song.

The auditory imagination which mute figures have the power of stimulating seems to be most active when the figures are in motion — at least that has been a psychological fact in my own experience. In my own collection of photographs I have a number of marines, instantaneous pictures of gigantic waves breaking on the rocky shelves on the coast of Maine; yet when I look at those pictures I do not vividly associate the sound with the phenomenon which I photographed. But when I see a motion picture of waves racing in from the offing, breaking wildly and rushing back beneath themselves I always hear in fancy the mighty roar of the sea. In my own case at least, movement suggests the unheard melody, whether the subject of the motion picture be a storm-swept forest, a church choir, or a hurdy-gurdy in a city street. In the Vatican is a famous group of statuary called " The Laocoön," which depicts the suffering of a father and his two sons, who are attacked by serpents. The cries of pain and despair we may imagine from the attitudes and facial expressions of the figures. At the "Arch of Triumph " in Paris is a sculptured group by Rude called "La Marseillaise," which represents the armoured figure of Liberty summoning a group of citizens to arms. We imagine from her dramatic gesture and specifically from the position of her lips that she is just sounding the vowel in the second word of " Aux armes, citoyens." The suggestive silence of arrested motion in these two groups of sculpture might have made a still stronger appeal to the imagination of sound if the figures could have been shown in progressive movement. At any rate the cinematic appeal to the auditory imagination is a new possibility of poetic expression which no serious photoplay-wright can afford to neglect. " High-brow " critics and apologists for the spoken drama have been known to sneer at the *silent* drama. Let the cinema composer attune their ears to the sounding beauties of that silence. Let him create out of this nothingness a new form of expression, until stillness becomes eloquent and the unheard melodies sweet.

In the mental play of imagining the sounds which must have accompanied the actions recorded on the screen, perhaps nothing is more fascinating than to shape the unheard but palpably significant words of the people in the pictures. Simple greetings and familiar formulas of speech we often grasp by lip reading, but around these easily recognized though unheard expressions, is a penumbra of conversation which we may vaguely reproduce in fancy. We often do it in real life. You look out through your window and see two gentlemen on the street. They meet, shake hands, speak a few words, and pass on. You do not hear a word; yet you can almost imagine what they say. You guess at it from the circumstances and from their general demeanour. Thus, too, on the screen the occasion of the action, the juxtaposition of the characters, and the context of the successive pictures enable us to infer the content of the conversation. Our intelligence is appealed to and we become, as it were, collaborators with the author. And each of us may have the joy of attributing his own phrases and formulas to the characters of the silent play. Suppose that we see an Italian garden as the dramatic setting in which a romantic lover is eloquent before his fair lady. His declarations are your words to you, and my words to me; what matters the difference in detail as long as he speaks the rapturous words of true love? If this trysting were to be set down in a book the words would be immutably there before our eyes, while our individual imagination would contribute the pictures. On the screen the magic play of pictures is the constant commodity, while toward these pictures the dramatic words leap silently from every spectator's fancy. "The nearest approach to cinematographed action is the dumb action of conventional stage pantomime." But in the case of the pure pantomime it should be observed that there is practically no appeal to auditory imagination because the actors deliberately act as though they were dumb. But in the photoplay the voices and sounds seem to be present though unheard by us. Here is a new and inviting problem to the dramatist, the problem of marshalling the strange forces of implied but unspoken words.

It is a still greater evidence of the cinema composer's skill if he can direct his characters so that we may imagine not only their dialog but their psychology as well even when there is no dialog. In everyday life we often find ourselves guessing at what somebody else is thinking. We observe a friend or an acquaintance involved in some little situation and we say, "I can just imagine what he thinks now." What he thinks may never find expression in words, but it is pleasant for us to speculate on what those words might possibly be. To imagine what a man thinks is sometimes more edifying than to listen to what he says, for is not language, especially language in polite society, often the means of concealing the actual state of mind? Oliver Wendell Holmes once said that when John talks to Thomas there are really six personalities distinctly to be recognized as taking part in the conversation, three Johns and three Thomases. The three Johns are (1) the real John, known only to his Maker; (2) John's ideal John; never the real one, and often very unlike him; (3) Thomas's ideal John; never the real John, nor John's John, but often very unlike either. In the same way there are three Thomases. Holmes might have multiplied the personalities; there was no logical necessity of stopping at six. But be that as it may, the zest of the verbal encounter between John and Thomas lies in the fact that neither one knows much about the other's personalities which lie beneath the surface of words. It would certainly be a dramatic error, a surrender to dull, matter of fact minds to represent these various personalities bodily or in respective speeches. That is, it would be an error if your aim were to stimulate the imagination of the spectator. Here again machinery is defeating art. In the motion pictures of today one of the ingenious and familiar devices is the double exposure which represents a single performer simultaneously in two different rôles or, better, in two personalities of the same character. By this means Dr. Jekyll can appear physically at one end of the room while Mr. Hyde appears during the same moment at the other. The effect is startling, it must be admitted; but the misleading implication is that there are two separate bodies as well as separate spiritual entities. On the stage, too, attempts have been made to enact literally the double personalities of a character. In Alice Gerstenberg's one act play *Overtones* we see two women, formerly more "chummy" than now, exchange polite or saccharine speeches across a tea table, while their suppressed personalities, represented by two other women up-stage, contradict these speeches with the pungent words of truth. This little play had a temporary stage success due to its novelty and humour, but as a work of art it is defective because it leaves nothing to the speculation or penetrative imagination of the spectator. It is a mistake to call upon language to express with mathematical precision the vague subtleties which should lie elusively between the lines.

Even these lines may be dispensed with in the new art of the picture play. The cinema composer ignores word language and uses instead the language of countenance and mien, the language of aspect and bearing and demeanour, of gesture and movement, the language of inanimate objects, of furniture and setting, of position and grouping and physical circumstance, the language of lights and shadows, and the magic of mechanical devices. This new language has syllables and phrases of a new texture. And the artist writer who would rise above mediocrity must combine these syllables and phrases so deftly that among and beneath them may be found a treasure trove of subtle suggestion, of things unformulated and unexpressed which shall quicken and vivify the imaginations of the multitudes of grateful spectators.

In the language of poetry we often find that the words mean much more than they actually denote, that they are enveloped, as it were, in a rich atmosphere of suggestion. Thus the words " Roman chariot " denote a vehicle for the conveyance of passengers, but no cultured mind would be content to pause on that limited meaning. The imagination, even of a school child, starting with these words could reconstruct the glamour and pomp of one of Cæsar's triumphs on a gala day in Rome. This quality of suggestion is known as the " connotation " of words. Cannot the cinema composer, the new poet of pictures, and not of words, develop a similar power of connotation? Cannot he too lash his steeds from a Roman chariot, or must he eternally crank a Ford car? The answer is plain; the cinema poet's power needs but to be exercised. The physical elements of a film picture may mean more to the imagination than they actually denote to the understanding. For example, a man in a dress suit connotes more than a man in an ordinary business suit; and a man in an eighteenth century costume connotes more than a man in a dress suit. So also a Turkish mosque or a Chinese pagoda connote more than a New Jersey church. And a king of Babylon connotes more than a negro prize fighter. There is a rich opportunity for the new poet of pictures to develop an imaginative style which shall distinguish him from the commonplace continuity writers, just as the styles of Byron and Keats distinguish them from Baedeker.

When we turn our attention from the elements of a photoplay to the composition as a whole we find ''that the various episodes and actions can be so arranged that much of the story is omitted or merely suggested, and must therefore be constructed by the imagination of the spectator.'' For example our fancy often leads us on beyond the end of a play. The impetus of our interest carries us into an imaginary sequel. We have become so familiar with our characters and so wrapped up in their lives that we are quite capable of continuing the tale even after the pictures have faded from the screen, and even though the solution of the particular dramatic problem before us has been complete. There are three other types of off-screen action which the spectator may imagine: the action which intervenes between successive episodes of the play, the action which is parallel to that shown on the screen, and the action which is antecedent to the beginning of the play.

A good example of intervening action may be found in *Milestones*, the stage play by Arnold Bennett and Edward Knoblauch. In the first act, laid in 1860, the young hero is a radical who believes that ships can be built of iron. He is in the ship building business with his father, who poohpoohs this newfangled idea. The consequence is that the son breaks away, starts a new firm and undertakes to build ships of iron. Twenty-five years pass before the second act opens. The hero has prospered, is the head of an interesting family, and has become a sturdy conservative, an unshakable man that England can depend upon. It is his turn to pooh-pooh the radical theories of the younger generation who believe that ships should be built of steel. Twenty-seven years pass, and the third act shows our venerable white-haired hero sitting before the fireplace. He has long since been knighted by the king, and, reminiscing over bygone days of brisk success, crabbedly seeks consolation for the losses that the steel built ships have forced upon him. The human interest in the play is heightened by the various love threads which are woven in, some of them all the way from 1860 to 1912. Here we see at once what a large, fascinating part of the play can be built in by the spectator himself by looking forward from one act and backward from the next. In the photoplay the various time lapses (discussed in the chapter on "Words") could often be utilized with a similar appeal to the imagination if only the photoplaywright were alert to the intellectual profit and constructed his episodes accordingly.

Earlier in this chapter we have referred to the part of a picture which is just outside the frame but which may be imagined inferentially from the part within the frame or on the screen. We shall now note that while the drama is being unfolded on the screen a parallel action may be taking place miles away and yet be inferentially kept in mind by the spectator. Such familiar devices as telegrams and letters keep us in touch with action which we cannot see, yet may visualize in our imaginations. This may be done in photoplay and stage play alike. But the photoplay has another interesting means of suggesting action not shown on the screen. ¶ This means, which the modern stage play cannot employ, is the paralleling of plots.❡ Let us say, for example, that scenes 23, 25, 27, and 29 of a play depict a German statesman in the Reichstag pleading for peace, while the alternate scenes 24, 26, and 28, depict his son, the captain of a submarine, attacking and sinking an English ocean liner. It is obvious that during scene 25 we would be remembering and visualizing the submarine, and during scene 28, the Reichstag. That is, the submarine action would have certain omitted, intervening sections which our imagination would supply subconsciously, while we were viewing the Reichstag action on the screen, and vice versa. This bridging of gaps is a pleasant exercise of the mind which the spectator should be allowed to indulge in.

❡The suggestion of antecedent action is not so easy in the photoplay as in the stage play.❡ Any one who is familiar with the structure of a Greek play knows that the action begins in the midst of a crisis and that the climax is not far off. As the play progresses we are given certain retrospective information until we are able to piece together perhaps years of action which leads up to the beginning of the play. Ibsen and most modern dramatists suggest antecedent action in a similar way. The effect is produced through the reminiscent narrative dialog of the characters. In so far as the photoplay possesses dialog it, too, can allude to the past. The earlier history of characters may be hinted at by close-ups of photographs, kodak prints, etc. Other means of retrospection can surely be devised in the course of experimentation with the motion picture as a medium of story telling. At any rate we may be sure that as photoplaywrights gain facility in handling their medium and raise higher standards of self criticism they will discover that it is bad art to project all the action of their plots upon the screen, that a part of every plot, whether antecedent, intervening, parallel, or subsequent action should be left to the imagination of those in the audience.

With complete mastery of cinema technique it would be possible even to construct a play in which one or more characters are entirely absent from the screen. This sounds like a severe strain upon the imagination, but such omissions have served a real artistic purpose in many classic examples of the stage drama. In Ibsen's *Ghosts,* to mention only one example, the character of Captain Alving, a happy-go-lucky rake, dominates the action and determines the tragedy of the entire play. Yet Captain Alving never appears on the scene; in fact, he is dead before the play opens. As a dramatic character, however, he is more potent dead than alive. There can be few in the audience who do not attempt to visualize his physical appearance. The photoplay can accomplish similar feats of technique when it masters its new language of signs and symbols and visible effects. Such obvious effects as a footprint in the sand, an arrow fired by an unseen enemy, a bomb thrown into a room from the darkness, the rays of a searchlight shooting in through a window, the shadow of a passerby who never enters,— all can start our fancies seeking the causes and shaping these causes into human beings.   Expectation, the fundamental element of dramatic interest, arises in our minds; and, before we know whether the suggested persons will ever appear or not, our imagination is at work creating their bodies and endowing them with souls.

This law of anticipative imagination is further recognized in stage plays when prominent characters are held off the stage until the second or third act in order to increase expectancy in the audience.   In Sheridan's *School for Scandal* the hero does not appear until the third scene of act three.   In Molière's *Tartufe* the hero does not appear until the third act.   In a photoplay, to a less degree, though with a similar appeal to the imagination, characters may be kept off the screen until they live in expectation before they actually materialize to the eye.   Setting and environment may be anticipated in a similar way.   Suppose we have a photoplay showing a few scenes of political and social life at Washington.   Then a Spanish diplomat announces that he is going back home to spend the summer in his castle in Spain.   Immediately everybody in the audience begins to imagine the castle, grounds, servants, furniture, and all.   In fact, the imagined castle is always more romantic and often more real than the one which is eventually thrown on the screen.

Thus we have suggested and analysed a dozen different ways of divesting the photoplay of that heavy materialism which weighs it down to the level of artifice and machinery.   If a photoplay is only a chain of motion photographs, it can never, for all its striking ingeniousness, entertaining novelty, and practical utility, rise into anything more than a mere pastime. And the thousands, perhaps millions, of people whose attentions are directed to that film will seek in vain the avenues which lead away from the humdrum of everyday life into the refreshing beauties of the realm of fancy. We have considered this subject from the angle of the spectator's interests. We have tried to discover certain archways of the ideal photoplay through which he might make imaginative incursions into an unexplored realm of art under the guidance of a new artist, the cinema composer.

CHAPTER VII

SYMBOLISM AND ALLEGORY

When we search around for ways and means of enlarging, enriching, and intensifying the expressive power of the motion picture we soon discover the language of symbolism and allegory. We observe the use of this fascinating language in painting, sculpture, architecture, literature, and music. But it is not in art alone that the symbolic object or act has been found necessary for complete human expression. Every day of our lives when other means fail we fall back upon symbols to express ourselves to each other. When I meet a friend who has been absent for some time I am glad to see him. My words tell him so. The tone of my voice and the smile on my face emphasize the words. And yet those three means of expression do not sufficiently convey my meaning. Therefore I clasp his hand. The shaking of hands is one of the most familiar of symbolic actions, so familiar, in fact, that we have long since forgotten that it is symbolic. It symbolizes a degree of unity and concord between two human beings which, we feel, could not otherwise be expressed with similar emphasis. When the social relation is still closer it may be symbolized by a kiss. Thus our social life is full of symbols, from the tipping of a hat to the wedding ring, from the gift of baby's spoon to the floral tribute at a grave. In political life, too, our expression resorts to symbols. The Stars and Stripes signify our country.   We mark our votes beneath some such emblem as the picture of an elephant or a donkey.   And we rise to the first strains of the National Anthem.   In religious expression the symbol, whether cross or crescent, is everywhere present and clearly understood.   In fact, all religious worship is symbolic, from the pagan sacrifice to baptism and the holy communion.   And the crucifix is as much a symbol as the Egyptian idol.   Thus we see that in the social, political, and religious phases of our everyday lives symbolism is a practical means of expression.

Symbolism in art is as old as art itself.   The key of life in the Egyptian monument, the halo in the religious painting, the Uncle Sam or the John Bull in the newspaper cartoon, all express something which the artist could not conveniently or successfully express in other terms.   Many of the subjects of sculpture are in themselves symbols, and were symbols in literature, that is in folk story, before the art of sculpture was developed.   Thus Venus symbolized love, Apollo, the sun, and Neptune, the sea, long before they were embodied in marble.   Music, too, is full of symbolism, all the way from the oldest melodies known, with their sexual significance, to the conventional symbolism of Wagnerian opera, wherein certain arrangements of notes are recognized by the initiate listener as symbolizing the sword, the magic flames, or Wotan.

If symbolism, then, is so widespread and useful in everyday life, and is so firmly established in the traditions of the elder arts, it follows that it should be mastered as a means of expression in the new art of the photoplay.   We have already said that the photoplay cannot achieve great triumph as art until it can make unforgettable impressions upon the spectator. Therefore the photoplay is especially in need of auxiliary forces that will help to deepen the main impression intended.

Let us define a symbol as a visible thing or act, an object, animal, person, device, or other visible stimulus which represents something else, by reason of natural aptness, of association, or of convention. Examples included under the various provisions of this definition are, the hand clasp, the lily, the serpent, Venus, the halo, the cross, and the colour red. Allegory might be defined as symbols in narrative action.

We have neither time nor space to make an analytic classification and enumeration of all the symbols that might possibly be used in the photoplay. And it is much more profitable for us to discuss the various functions and methods of applying symbolism in the photoplay. It must, of course, be remembered at the outset that, while we insist that many photoplays could be strengthened in dramatic and pictorial appeal by the use of symbolism, we do not insist that all photoplays can be thus strengthened. We merely recommend symbolism, as we have recommended pictorial composition and camera magic, as one of the elements of the cinema composer's medium, to be used at his own discretion as an artist.

Symbols or symbolic acts may be used to identify persons in a play, to indicate or emphasize the character of persons, to express meanings which could not otherwise be expressed, to emphasize meanings simultaneously expressed in other terms, and to emphasize the plot as such by reinforcing its significance. Furthermore, a character may sometimes himself be a symbol, and a plot may be all allegory from beginning to end.

The identification of a person by the use of a symbol may occur under various dramatic circumstances. For example, in a scene during the first centuries of the Christian era two Romans, strangers to each other, meet on the sea beach. They are within sight and hearing of Roman officers. One of the strangers, casually stirring the sand with his stick, draws the design of a fish, thus immediately revealing himself to the other as a Christian, because the fish was the secret symbol of the Christians. Here the dramatic circumstance was the need of secrecy. Another circumstance might be that of a person trying unsuccessfully to hide his identity. In the " Walpurgis-Nacht " of *Faust* Mephistopheles is one of the revellers, masquerading as a man. But one of the shrewd old hags recognizes him by his cloven hoof, which is one of the symbolic attributes of the devil. Or a symbol may be used for identification simply because the author finds it more convenient than any other expression. Thus the early Christian painters established the convention of identifying the Nazarene as the Son of God by painting an aureole, or halo, around his head. Griffith in his *Intolerance* used a similar device in the scene of the Marriage of Cana, where Christ is easily singled out from the others by the radiant light in the shape of a cross, which he seems to project from himself as he walks along. The device was pictorially effective, but was, of course, an anachronism, since the cross was not a Christian symbol until the Saviour had been crucified upon it. We may mention in passing that the painters represented God the Father by the symbol of a hand reaching down out of a cloud, a tradition which may have inspired Rodin to a variant use in his piece of sculpture " The Hand of God," in which a mighty hand reaching up from a solid base holds within its grasp a human pair just emerging from a shapeless lump of earth. One dramatic use of a symbol is for the identification of a person who is not yet aware of his own identity. Thus, for example, in the Famous Players film adaptation of *The Girl Philippa,* Philippa, a foundling, is of unidentified parentage until we see a package of things found with her. This package contains a beautiful cloak with the fleur-de-lis of France embroidered in one corner. When we see this emblem we realize that Philippa is of princely origin. Of symbolic identification in humorous design the newspaper cartoonists furnish innumerable examples. In all the cases of symbolism which we have just described or alluded to it should be noticed that the symbol is decorative as well as useful, that its value is pictorial as well as descriptive.

The delineation of character in the photoplay is especially difficult, as we shall see in a later chapter, because of the substantial absence of words, and because of other limitations of the motion picture. But the art of symbolism may be called in to emphasize the character of a person who is otherwise described by his acts or by his pantomimic expression. The symbolic costume is one of the oldest of pictorial and dramatic conventions. An angel or an innocent girl is draped in white, while the devil or a villain wears black. Now, as a matter of fact, we may have seen villains in white flannel suits, and we may have known angelic girls who often wore black, yet the symbolic values of white and black in picture and story have been so deeply rooted in our minds that we would surely be shocked if we saw a play in which the villain, dressed in immaculate white, exercised his evil influence upon a pure maiden armoured with virtue and deep black robes.   Character may further be emphasized by the accompaniment of some object.   Thus in Italian paintings an armful of lilies held by the white-robed Madonna at the Annunciation emphasize her purity and virginity.   Perhaps the lily is no purer chemically than, say, a hollyhock, yet in the picture described not even an infant would be satisfied by the hollyhock as a substitute.   In a similar way such a symbol as a crucifix or a rosary would emphasize the character of the person connected with it.   A cinematic expedient for stressing the nature of a person is the symbolic setting.   For example, in the photoplay *Purity* a man who is to be thought of as the devil personified is shown in one place quite at home beside a growth of cactus and a nest of writhing serpents. Another, more arbitrary device is to be found in the photoplay adaptation of *Trilby,* where at one moment we see a huge spider's web stretching across the screen and presently perceive at its centre the face of Svengali, his wicked eyes searching eagerly for prey. Still another fanciful device is the symbolic shadow, used, for example, when a fickle-hearted woman comes upon the scene holding her draperies in such a way that the shadow thrown before her is in the form of a butterfly, or when some saintly man stands with outstretched arms so that his shadow makes the sign of the cross.   All these auxiliaries in the delineation of character are valuable factors in the motion picture because they operate simultaneously with other terms of expression. They throw light on character at the very same moment when it is being revealed by deed or pantomimic expression. Furthermore, the symbols named operate instantly. The spectator of average intelligence can interpret them immediately without dictionary or teacher. This is due partly to the natural aptness of the symbol or its familiar association, and partly to the fact that the language we speak is full of symbolism. We constantly hear such expressions as "pure as a lily," "black as sin," "vile as a serpent," "a social butterfly," etc. A final resource of symbolism for emphasizing character is the title of a play, which may present to our imagination a symbol nowhere used in the play. There is obvious descriptive symbolism in such titles as *The Serpent, The Vampire, The Black Butterfly,* and *Damaged Goods.*

A third use of symbolism is the expression of ideas, meanings, propositions which would otherwise have to be conveyed in words, or for which not even words would be adequate. The American Indians often resorted to symbolic actions when they had no other means of communicating with the white settlers. One of our school histories tells of an Indian chief who sent an ultimatum to a settler in the form of a bundle of arrows wrapped in a snake skin. The white man answered symbolically by returning the snake skin filled with powder and shot. Such an action is sufficiently expressive, and is far more pleasing to the eye and to the imagination than an exchange of documents thrown on the screen and held there while the children beside us carefully spell out the words. A search of Indian history and lore will reveal many a symbolic act, such as smoking the peace pipe or burying the hatchet, which could be given narrative or descriptive value in a photoplay.   Any means of effective expression which will help us to dispense with words is to be welcomed, because the photoplay cannot be developed into great art as long as it remains hybrid, half literary and half pictorial." Therefore even when words might be used it is better to express the same idea in deed, pantomime, or in symbolism, or in all three simultaneously." What can words on the screen add to the picture of a young man placing an engagement ring on his sweetheart's finger and sealing the compact with kisses?   Or what words are really necessary when a vanquished officer goes through the ceremony of surrendering his sword to his vanquisher?

Abstract ideas have long been represented in paintings by the use of symbols.   Thus the anchor symbolizes hope, the lily, purity; and a nude woman holding a mirror up to the beholder symbolizes truth.   The traditional method of representing truth was adopted in *Hypocrites*, a rather crudely constructed photoplay containing many beautiful elements.   Unfortunately the charm and significance of this play was lost to multitudes of art lovers because of the vulgar advertising designed to give the public the notion that *Hypocrites* was a pornographic exhibition.   We shall give a general outline of the plot when we come to the discussion of allegory.   The abstract idea of conscience or remorse has been symbolized in many ways in literature.   An impressive example is Poe's *The Tell-Tale Heart,* in which a murderer is driven to confession because he imagines that he hears the beating of the dead man's heart.   But a symbolic sound, especially an imaginary one, has, of course, no cinematic value. However, some inventive cinema composer may find a cinematic effect which will be as expressive in pictures as Poe's conception is in words. *The Secret of the Swamp,* a photoplay already alluded to, was a step in the right direction. A planter shooting at a neighbour's cow believes that he has shot the neighbour by accident, and that the man has crawled off to the swamp to die. The next day the planter sees turkey buzzards soaring above the swamp as if on the scent of a dead body. These black buzzards become, as it were, the symbols of remorse. Their shadows fall across his path as he crosses his own yard, and their forms are seen dimly in the room where he tries to sleep. He is driven to confess murder, only to find at the end of the story that the neighbour is still alive and was not even grazed by the bullet. All this loses in value when described in words but has considerable symbolic expression when seen in motion pictures.

What one character thinks of another can sometimes be expressed in symbolism as eloquently as in words. A good example of this may be found in the screen adaptation of *Trilby.* Trilby is an artist's model, a picturesque woman of unquestionably questionable past. Little Billee is shocked when he finds her posing in the nude for a fellow artist, yet he is madly in love with her and wants to marry her. His attitude toward her is beautifully shown in the scene where he is shown lovingly painting a picture of the Madonna. His model is Trilby, white-robed, with lilies in her arms. The significance was undoubtedly clear to the audience, yet no psychological analysis in words could have been more subtle.

Sometimes a symbolic action may be so devised that it is really a plot in miniature.   It can then be used to emphasize a dramatic plot by paralleling its action or expressing its meaning in other terms.   This symbolic plot in miniature has long been used in stage drama. Let us give an example of the dumb show, as it was called, which preceded the first act of *Gorboduc*, printed in 1565.   We give it in its original quaint form.   " First the musicke of violenze began to play, during which came vpon the stage sixe wilde men, clothed in leaues; of whom the first bare in his necke a fagot of small stickes, which they all, both seuerally and together, assayed with all their strengthes to breake, but it could not be broken by them.   At the length, one of them plucked out one of the stickes and brake it, and the rest plucking out all the other stickes one after an-other did easely breake them, the same being seuered, which, being conioyned, they had before attempted in vaine, After they had this done, they departed the stage; and the musicke ceased.   Hereby was signified that a state knit in vnitie doth continue strong against all force, but being diuided is easely destroyed."*Pictorially this naïve bit of pantomime has no great value, but it was undoubtedly expressive to the spectators and helpful in emphasizing to them the dramatic significance of the plot which was presently unfolded to them in the long, blank verse speeches of the tragic actors.* Today the dumb show, or symbolic pantomime, survives with greatly expanded and constantly expanding powers of expression.   Symbolism on the screen has greater scope than symbolism in painting because it includes symbols in action, and "has greater scope than symbolism in the stage drama because it can bring together symbols of greater number and variety, and can rely on camera magic for many startling effects." A recent photoplay entitled *Enlighten Thy Daughter* emphasized its plot by a symbolic pantomime which would have been impossible in stage drama and could not have been suggested in a single painting. The photoplay began with the picture of an idyllic clearing which extended to the edge of a high cliff. Upon this scene was faded in the caption " The Heights of Purity." Then the scene shifts downward to a chaotic mass of broken rocks at the foot of the cliff, and the caption " The Depths of Shame " is faded in. We now return to the clearing and see two young girls dressed in white and blindfolded walking toward the edge of the cliff. Just as they reach the brink an arm reaches out and removes the bandage from the eyes of one of the girls. The other walks innocently to her ruin. We see her take the fatal step and fall to destruction at the foot of the cliff. The symbolism was instantly understood by the audience and will be remembered by them long after the stirring plot of the play itself has been forgotten.

The pantomime just described was, of course, purposely conceived and deliberately executed by those who produced the play. Its dramatic function was obvious, and could have been no more so if it had been preceded by the caption " Symbolic Prologue." Its value lay in this very obviousness, and in its detached parallelism with the play. Another, more subtle use of a symbolic parallel occurs when a bit of natural action within the play itself is so treated that it assumes a suggestive meaning over and above its primary pictorial or dramatic meaning. In the photoplay *Unto the Fourth Generation* there was a bit of casual stage business which had merely a decorative value, but which by a slight shifting could have been invested with a subtle, impressive symbolism, paralleling the significance of the entire play. The main story involved a rake who was very much in the power of his mistress, a woman of the vampire type. The rake was the guardian of a sweet, innocent girl, whom he eventually marries. The mistress immediately begins evil machinations against the girl-wife, partly because of jealousy and partly because she desires to get the man's money. The bad woman triumphs unmistakably over the good woman, who ends her days disowned and blind in an asylum. In one of the scenes of this play the girl-wife is shown standing at a window plucking the petals out of a rose until she has quite destroyed it. Now whoever directed this play showed an amazing power of resisting the temptation to produce a beautiful dramatic effect. Or is it possible that he did not realize that the business of the rose should have been given to the vampire? She should, of course, have been shown talking with the rake, telling lies about his young wife, meanwhile ruthlessly, casually, plucking a white rose to pieces, the petals falling to the floor and left unnoticed beneath her feet. Symbolism of this kind is especially desirable in the photoplay because it is unobtrusive and organic, operating on the eye of the spectator simultaneously with other means of dramatic expression.

The device of putting a symbolic setting into action

is another means of emphasizing a plot. Setting is made highly symbolic by Poe in *The Fall of the House of Usher.* The story tells of the tragic end of the last two members of the family of Usher. The narrator of the story begins by describing the melancholy impression made upon him by his first view of the house in which the Ushers lived. It was a decayed old building with bleak walls, and vacant eye-like windows, standing on the edge of a dark tarn. That it was doomed to fall was evident from the wide fissure which had sprung open from top to bottom of the front wall. The death of the demented Roderick Usher takes place during a violent storm, and the narrator riding away from the scene of the tragedy, looks back in time to see the house crumble and fall and disappear completely beneath the waters of the tarn; which "closed sullenly and silently over the fragments of the ' House of Usher.' " This story should be read and studied carefully, for it is a good illustration of the art of making one effect reinforce another until a single, deep, abiding impression results. And it is just this art, the art of making many things work together toward one end, which the cinema composers must master.

In another department of literature, the drama, Ibsen can teach us many a lesson in the method of deepening an impression by the use of symbolism. In *Ghosts,* for example, the orphanage, called "Captain Alving's Foundation " is built in memory of the rake from whom a terrible disease was inherited by Oswald. Thus the orphanage and Oswald are both founded on evil. The orphanage is not insured; neither is Oswald. The village pastor blesses the orphanage, as he had years before blessed the union of Oswald's father and mother. The orphanage burns. Oswald, commenting upon it, says: "Everything will burn. All that recalls father's memory is doomed. Here am I, too, burning down." And when the final curtain falls the poor boy is a maniac, his life slowly burning out. Thus the story of the building parallels the story of the hero; the symbolic setting in action emphasizes the plot of the drama.

The plot of a play may further be emphasized by a symbolic title, particularly a title which contains an implied allegory paralleling the main import of the plot. One of Bernard Shaw's plays represents the story of a London professor of phonetics who believes that any girl of low birth and breeding could pass in society as a duchess, provided she were taught to speak the English language according to the standards of cultivated society. He tries the experiment on a flower girl whom he picks up on the streets, and is so successful in the transformation that he himself falls in love with the girl. Such a development in the action was suggested by the play's title, *Pygmalion*, to any one at all familiar with Greek mythology, because Pygmalion was the mythical character who fell in love with an ivory statue he had made. Thus to a fairly large percentage of people who see Shaw's comedy of real Londoners the plot is anticipated, emphasized, and, after a time, recalled by a single word, by a symbol that reminds them of a parallel plot devised thousands of years ago by the myth makers of Greece. Less fantastic symbols are employed and have perhaps greater expressiveness in the titles of such plays as Zangwill's *The Melting Pot,* Pinero's *The Thunderbolt,* Bennet and Knoblauch's *Milestones,* and Brieux' *The Cog-wheels.*

A unique opportunity for symbolism in the photo-play is to be found in the decoration of subtitles, or captions, which are to be read by the audience.   For example, in Ince's cinema spectacle of war and peace *Civilization* the reading matter thrown upon the screen was decorated with simple drawings of cannon, swords, the crown of thorns, the dove of peace, etc., according to the significance of the story at that par-ticular point.   We approve of such symbolism thor-oughly, providing these graphic designs do not distract from the legend, or providing they really are decora-tive and really emphasize the meaning of the words. In the photoplay *The Dumb Girl of Portici* the sym-bols were very distracting, because they were mo-tion pictures of objects, such as veils, gloves, etc., in motion, and it was very difficult to tell just what the objects were and just what their motions signified. In the photoplay *The Poor Little Rich Girl* we find symbolic drawings which were totally unnecessary, thereby demanding our attention in vain.   When a plumber comes in to fix a kitchen sink, it surely is not necessary to surround his remarks projected on the screen with drawings of plumber's tools.   This sort of art reminds us of other photoplays where the screened dialog of telephone conversations was surrounded by drawings of telephone fixtures, telephone poles, and wires.   Yet these inanities may do some good if they serve to fix our minds on what might be done if the cinema composer had enough sense of art to designate the proper symbols to accompany his captions and could find some one in the studio with enough skill and taste to execute the designs so that the symbols might please the eye while reinforcing the meaning of the words or action. A great number of symbols, such as the anchor of hope, the scales of justice, the torch of learning, which have long been the stock of painters, but are not easily available for dramatic action, might thus find a new use in an art which needs enlarged powers of expression and emphasis.

❡ We have enumerated and tried to illustrate the various methods of applying symbolism as an auxiliary force in the photoplay. ❡ It may be used to identify, describe, or emphasize a character, to emphasize words or actions, or to take their place in the expression of ideas, and to interpret or parallel a plot. ❡ We now come to a discussion of symbolism which is self-relying instead of auxiliary to some other means of expression. A character may be a symbol through and through, and have no other interest for us except the interest in the thing symbolized. And a plot may be an allegory from beginning to end thus fixing our attention, not on itself, but rather on the dramatic things and actions symbolized.

It is natural for a primitive people, untravelled, unlearned, unscientific, to think of their surroundings, the sky, the sea, the woods, the earth, as well as of the unseen forces, in terms of themselves and their own lives. But they are not content to attribute human personality to unseen forces and to non-human things; they soon invent persons to represent them, half believing that these persons have existence, each in some appropriate realm. Hence in Greek mythology we have Jupiter, furious as the thunderbolt, Neptune, dangerous as the sea, Venus, passionate as love, and Diana, cool as the moon.   But a character who has only one single trait, only a single string to his harp, becomes insufferably dull as a companion, and impossible as an object of contemplation.   If the myth makers of Greece had stopped with the attribution of a single trait to each character, those figures would not have lived so long in the stories of the race.   But they did not stop.   In the course of time any given symbolic character was invested with new attributes until he or she became as complex and interesting as any human being in history or fiction.   Diana, for example, was first conceived as the goddess of the moon, then, because of various superstitions connected with the moon, she was thought of as the goddess of fertility, of huntsmen, of wild animals, of fishermen, of virginity, of music and the dance, and of death.   In these various rôles, all coalescing, she developed various traits and mental capacities and became the central figure in many symbolic legends.   And while she grew up into an interesting personality she also enriched her symbolic connotation. Therefore to the Greeks she was neither too obvious and simple as a symbol, nor too colourless as a character.

"Now the cinema composer who creates a symbolic character should endeavour to make it a genuine character as well as a symbol, or he should devise a plot which will be interesting despite the fact that it contains lay figures instead of real characters." One single trait is not enough to make a character.   Purity, Envy, or Jealousy do not suddenly become characters by acquiring arms, legs, and the power of locomotion.   As soon as the spectator finds out that Purity is one hundred percent pure, and will for ever remain so, he ceases to be fascinated by Purity herself. But if he discovers that she is only ninety-nine percent pure, and one percent proud, or jealous, or mischievous, he will look upon her as a person, and will be alert to the possibility of seeing her involved in interesting action. If there is a chance for the unexpected there may be suspense; and suspense is the fundamental element in a plot. But if the symbol in human form is Folly, Abstinence, Mercy, Revenge, Justice, Falsehood, or some such abstraction, the spectator is not allowed to speculate concerning the future actions of these figures. He knows that Mercy will not be revengeful, and that Justice will not be false. However, as we shall show in the chapter on " Dramatic Appeal," there are various kinds of suspense, and it is possible for a spectator to be held by plot interest even when he knows what the characters really are and what they must inevitably do. The spectator, knowing *what* will happen, may still be kept in suspense as to *when* it will happen, and *how* it will happen. **

With these considerations in mind let us examine a few allegorical plays, to see wherein their plot value resides. One of the most successful of the English morality plays produced during the fifteenth and sixteenth centuries is *Everyman,* printed in 1529. The plot is briefly as follows: God sends his messenger Death to tell Everyman that he must prepare for his last pilgrimage. Everyman tries in vain to have the pilgrimage postponed, but gets no concession except that he may take along with him any companions who care to follow. But he does not have much luck in getting up a party. Fellowship, Kindred, and Cousin are not interested in the trip. Riches only mocks the idea.   In despair he turns to his long-neglected friend Good Deeds, who promises to help him.   She secures him a guide in her sister Knowledge ("the discreet and learned advice which religion has at her service"). Everyman now goes to Confession, where he receives the jewel Penance (the sacrament).   He then sets forth clad in the garment Contrition, and accompanied by Beauty, Strength, Discretion, and Five Senses.   But at the sight of the grave these companions forsake him. Only Good Deeds and Knowledge are steadfast to the end, when Everyman sinks into the grave and commends his spirit to God.

When we test this allegory for plot value we see that every action planned by any one in the play has an outcome or consequence which the spectator can predict with certainty.   However, though the spectator knows what the dramatic figures will do, he does not know what they will say, what excuses they will invent for their pre-established actions, or how they will look when the moment of action comes.   A further element of suspense for us today consists in our being alertly expectant of the grim poetic touches and the quaint language of the play.

When a skilled contemporary dramatist writes an allegorical play he does not like to use label-names, because he realizes that they tend to dehumanize the characters and reveal the plot too soon.   Therefore Maeterlinck calls death The Intruder in the play of that name, and Jerome alludes to his hero, who symbolizes Christ, simply by the nickname "The Third Floor Back" in the play *The Passing of the Third Floor Back*.   Kennedy in his *The Servant in the*

House suggests the symbolism of his central figure by the title of the play and by the name Manson, which is, of course, derived from the expression "the Son of Man." Mr. Kennedy's play is one of the most effective of contemporary stage allegories, and we recommend a careful perusal of it to any one interested in the use of symbolism.

Before going any further in the discussion of allegorical plays we must draw a sharp distinction between a sermon or treatise in dramatic form and a drama which has an underlying philosophy or preachment. The primary aim of one is to teach; the primary aim of the other is to entertain. Now practically all allegories are of the first type. They are deliberately designed to present an argument, impress a doctrine, or point a moral. Their symbolism is used to emphasize a lesson, rather than to deepen a dramatic thrill or to brighten a dramatic beauty. The lessons of *Everyman* are obvious from the synopsis we have given. The lesson of *The Passing of the Third Floor Back* is that Christianity can make bad men better and happier. The lesson of *The Servant in the House* is that the church can be regenerated only in the spirit, and by the teaching, of Christ himself. But playgoers will not gladly invest in tickets with the prospect of being preached at or argued with. They will not eagerly swallow a play if they know that it is essentially a pill. Therefore, as a medical pill must sometimes be sugar coated, so a didactic pill must always be art coated. If an author has a message to deliver or a lesson to teach in the form of allegory he should strive to make his allegory so attractive as dramatic entertainment that the audience either will get the lesson without knowing it or will endure the lesson for the sake of the entertainment.

Thus although Maeterlinck's *The Blue Bird* symbolizes the familiar Sunday School moral that true happiness consists in being unselfish, yet it furnishes delightful entertainment to any one, young or old, because of the charm, whimsicality, and refreshing originality which envelop the moral. The play tells the story of two children, Mityl and Tyltyl, who dream that they are on a romantic search for the Blue Bird, symbol of happiness. Under the guidance of Light they search in the land of Memory, in the region of Night, in the forest, in the graveyard, and in the kingdom of the Future, but everywhere in vain. Finally when they wake up in their humble cottage they are addressed by a woman, a neighbour, who comes to borrow their caged turtle dove, for which her sick child has been asking. As they give up their bird they discover that it has turned a deep blue. This is the main story and the main symbolism. But there is much entertainment and symbolic meaning in subsidiary things, such as the delightful nonsense in the personified Bread, Sugar, Milk, Cat, and Dog; the pictorial phenomena in the graveyard with the message "There are no dead!", and the wistful poetry of the souls of the unborn children. The symbolism is everywhere evident, yet it is so artistically presented that no spectator could ever yawn and say, "Dear, dear, what a dull text, and what an old, old story."

We know that Maeterlinck wrote *The Blue Bird* for performance as spoken drama, but it is easy to see that fundamentally the play is a cinematographic conception. Its dream and visions, its many settings and fanciful wandering, its transformation of things into human beings, its dramatization of animals and natural settings, its symbols in action, all constitute the very effects which can be produced more successfully on the screen than anywhere else in art. We firmly believe that new opportunities will discover new genius. If Maeterlinck still prefers to express himself in words, some new Maeterlinck will arise and express himself masterfully in the motion picture.

Up to the present writing no really artistic allegory has appeared on the screen. But an interesting attempt was made in *Hypocrites,* a five reel photoplay written and directed by Lois Weber. In the first part of the story Friar Gabriel makes a statue of a nude woman to represent Truth. This he presents to the city. But at the unveiling of the statue the populace, shocked at the nakedness of Truth, destroy the statue and slay the sculptor. Hundreds of years later Gabriel is re-incarnated as a modern minister of the gospel. In a sermon on hypocrisy he offends his congregation so that they turn against him for his candour. In his despair he is inspired by the visionary figure of Truth, a nude woman. She leads him through the Gates of Truth and takes him through the world revealing hypocrisy everywhere. Politics and law are corrupt, society is degenerate, family life is unwholesome, love is sensual, and religion is a sham. One section of the film symbolizes the difficulty of following truth. We see Truth climbing a steep hill beckoning all to follow. The rich man cannot follow because his money bags are too heavy; the society woman cannot follow for fear of ruining her elegant clothes; other people in various walks of life do not even try to follow; the only ones who are able to follow Truth to the heights are Gabriel and a modest young woman, one of his parishioners. Presently we are back in the church, which is empty except for two people, Gabriel, who has evidently dreamed the modern allegory, and the young woman in the pew, she alone remaining when all the rest had fled at the minister's words of truth.

Hypocrites has many faults and many merits. It has many beautiful pictures and many charming bits of symbolism. But it is crude in construction and lacks consistency. It is neither consistently improbable nor consistently probable. It does not have the organized system of improbabilities which we see in *The Blue Bird,* nor the rationalized allegory which we see in *The Servant in the House,* where real and natural actions and things have been invested with a symbolic meaning. For example, it is not probable that a Wall Street man would carry his money in bags over his shoulder, but it is extremely probable that his wife would hesitate to climb a rough hill path for fear of tearing her dress and scratching her shoes. Furthermore, although the nude in this photoplay was treated in a delicate and thoroughly inoffensive way, and can always be so treated in the motion pictures, The Society of the Daughters of Concealment to the contrary notwithstanding, yet the idea of a frock-coated minister pursuing a nude woman through the Jersey woods does not in itself appropriately symbolize the quest for truth.

Thus we have shown throughout this chapter the difficulty as well as the effectiveness of applying symbolism as a means of expression in the photoplay. We should always remember that the aim of every artist should be to economize the appreciator's attention, to give him the maximum of art with the minimum demand of effort. We have shown that symbolism does economize the appreciator's attention by expressing clearly what could not otherwise be so clearly expressed, and by emphasizing what could not otherwise be sufficiently emphasized. We have already said in an earlier chapter that the photoplay needs to have considerable surface value because of its transitory existence before the eyes of the spectator. Symbolism in the photoplay, therefore, should be instantly active. It should clarify or emphasize something the moment it is seen. In other words, the symbol should be self-explanatory. To compose a photoplay in which the symbolism meant nothing until it was itself explained, would be like writing a story in a code which could not be read without a cipher. We do not insist that the spectator must be conscious of the fact that the expression is symbolic, but we do insist that he must get the symbolized meaning even though he get it subconsciously. He must be made to feel the dramatic effect even though he does not understand how it is produced.

The use of obscure or mystic symbolism may be more justifiable in the stage drama which is meant to be read as well as acted, because the reader at least may pause and study with his finger on the page. He may even turn to other writings about the very play he is reading. No one should undertake to read the plays of Ibsen without first reading through Jennette Lee's beautiful analysis of his symbolism in her book *The Ibsen Secret*. The very title and existence of Miss

Lee's book is proof that Ibsen's symbolism is not self-explanatory and not instantly active to the appreciator. In Ibsen's case the obscure and submerged symbolism is no great drawback, because his plays are tremendously impressive even to the one who does not see the parallel meanings.   In fact, the reserved meanings are a gain, because as one reads an Ibsen play over and over again he learns the Ibsen language, which reveals an ever increasing store of riches.   But under present conditions of photoplay exhibition it would be unsafe for the cinema composer to withhold or conceal any substantial part of his treasure; perhaps he may do so under the conditions of possible permanence and study of the photoplay which may come about in the future.

We opened our discussion of symbolism by pointing to its use in the elder arts, we have shown how much of this symbolism can be used and even given new values in the motion picture.   We shall end by hoping to see new symbolism in the new medium of the photoplay.   Ingenious cinema composers will invent new symbols especially expressive in the motion picture and possible only on the screen.   Symbolism in painting and sculpture and architecture and literature was old when Wagner came along and created a new symbolism in his arrangement of consecutive musical notes.   Why should not the next innovation be in the medium of consecutive motion pictures?

CHAPTER VIII

DRAMATIZING A NATURAL SETTING

"A TREMENDOUS resource which distinguishes the photoplay from all other narrative and dramatic arts is the possibility of representing an action in its natural setting." For the first time in the history of the arts which mimic human happenings it has become possible for the spectator to go to the very spot where the action takes place. This privilege could never be conveniently afforded the audience of the spoken drama. The appreciator of the stage play must sit in his chair while the dramatist calls in the action from its natural environment, confines it under the roof of the theatre, and represents it amid imitated settings of canvas and *papier-mâché*. The appreciator of the photoplay may sit no less comfortably in his chair, and yet, through the magic power of the camera, may follow the action wherever it goes, into the remotest heights and depths, and into the smallest nooks and crannies of the world. If it is natural that a fairy story should take place in a forest we may go there to witness the action. Keeping just behind the camera, we may skip with the elves over brooks in which real water trickles over real stones, and scamper away with them among real trees swaying in a real wind. Thus, too, if our hero is a mediaeval knight we may ride with him over the drawbridge and beneath the portcullis into the castle. If he is an aviator we soar with him among the clouds;

if he is a diver we sink with him to submarine depths. Wherever the hero goes, we go; whatever he sees, we see. This possibility of following the story in its natural environment is a new resource of the cinema composer. He may conjure with a new appeal to the spectator; he may give the story a unique reality which the stage never could give it; he may utilize the artistic value which the real setting may have in itself; and he may even harness the natural setting and make it tell a part of his story.

It is obvious that by the term "natural setting" we include something more than that part of nature which has been untouched or unmodified by man. The manmade pyramids, an Italian garden, or a Western ranch may be as natural a setting for one story as the ocean or a glacier for another. The term is meant to be self-defining. The place where a fictitious action would naturally happen if it were real life is the natural setting of that action. In discussing the psychology of the spectators we have already spoken of the new appeal which the screen play affords by bringing us into the presence of real nature. We spoke then of the pleasure of the eye in beholding the beauty of a natural subject, and of the self emotion which the spectator experiences in the illusion of photographic contact with real nature. We spoke also of the informational value, the satisfaction of curiosity, which the spectator gets from viewing scenes which he might never be allowed to visit in reality. All of these appeals may be called absolute appeals, because they exist for the spectator quite regardless of whether the setting is related to a story or not. They may be present in the "scenics" or "educational films" which do not endeavour to represent dramatic incident or situation. But if the cinema composer can mobilize this enjoyment of nature and natural setting, can harness it and subordinate it in the service of his dramatic situation and plot, he will do something which the playwright of words cannot do, and will in this respect make the photoplay more expressive than the stage play."

When we analyse our enjoyment of nature which is shown on the screen we find that the appeal lies in three phases, in the permanent aspects of nature, in the phenomena of nature, and in the life of animals. The most familiar appeal is in the permanent aspects. To us busy city-dwelling or village-haunting folk there is something refreshing in the motion picture of the sparkling brook for ever hurdling its way over water-worn stones, something reminiscent of boyhood or of yesterdays on vacation. In the mighty rush of a waterfall, in the endlessly undulating billows of the sea, in the wild white fury of the surf, there is beauty for the eye and the emotion of awe for the soul. There is something arresting, too, in the long thin ripples of a placid lake or the crowding ice floes of a majestic river. Even when the element of movement is slight or absent from the subject we enjoy the motion picture of nature. We love the long white sweep of drifted snow among the dark spruce trees or the boldly jutting crags of a canyon. Our eyes follow with pleasure the smooth dip of a valley, or the slow curves of the foothills on the horizon. There is delight for the eye in the wonderful play of light and shade massed in the quivering shadows among the birches, in the sharp sun peeping out from the edges of a cloud, and in the deep silhouette of scraggly oaks against a sunset sky. These and hundreds of other permanent aspects of nature can easily be found by the photographer and can be woven like rich threads into the fabric of the photoplay.

The phenomena of nature are more rare and are not so easily captured by the camera. But when they are caught and projected on the screen the results are impressive. Millions of us may see accurately through the lens of the camera something which we would never in our lives see in any other way. Perhaps the most picturesque natural phenomenon is a volcanic eruption. When we see it on the screen we discover that the sides of the mountain are not as steep as in the pictures of our geographies, that the dark column rising from the volcano's mouth is more flattened and slow-moving than we had expected; and yet we are spellbound by the cinema record because we know that we are seeing something real. And our imagination begins all over again weaving the destinies of the real people who actually live within the shadow of this furious giant. Less picturesque, though no less tragic in their bearing on human happiness, are the floods which so frequently rise in the rivers of the Middle West. To see a river turn into an ocean during a week end, to see corn fields and farm steads and villages disappear beneath its surface is an experience which no spectator ever forgets. It is a picture which can never be utilized dramatically anywhere except in the photoplay. Another phenomenon of nature, common in the Middle West, which might be difficult to manage in a photoplay, but would make an unforgettable picture, is the tornado. The black, funnel-shaped cloud reaching down from the heavens to mark a path of destruction over the earth, though defying rehearsal, might some day be filmed by a patient camera man, and would undoubtedly produce a dramatic effect dear to the hearts of producers and " movie fans." The camera man might sail the seas for years before he could photograph a terrifying typhoon, or he might live in the Alps a decade before he could photograph an avalanche, but imagine what a strong pictorial climax he might be able to furnish to some cinema tragedy of avenging fate.

An interesting condition of photoplay production is the fact that even if a dramatic effect can be produced only once, that is enough for the photoplay. The effect does not have to be so conceived and contrived that it can be reproduced once or twice a day as in the stage play, in an opera, or in a hippodrome spectacle. In the photoplay therefore even an accident can be dramatized. And the producer who wants to realize the remotest possibility of cinema production may capture and subdue and dramatize the phenomena or seeming accidents of nature herself. But whether the phenomenon of nature is dramatized well or badly or not at all, the absolute appeal to the eyes and emotions of the spectator is still there and constitutes a new dramatic or narrative medium which only the cinema composer can manipulate.

The motion picture of animals always elicit the spectator's applause. One of the producers in New York City is so dependent on this appeal that he never fails to drag in two or three different kinds of animals whether they have any conceivable connection with the photoplay or not. When criticized for his haphazard way of constructing photoplays, he replies that he doesn't care about logic or art so long as people find something they like in his pictures. We shall point out a little later in this chapter how animals may be dramatized in a photoplay, but for the present let us see why people are so fond of animals on the screen. First of all the picture carries with it some of the appeal which the subject has in real life. We feel affection for our pets, dogs, kittens, and squirrels. We feel a certain, perhaps subconscious, yet real, gratitude toward the brute beings, cows, horses, and sheep, that help support our lives. We experience a feeling of wonder at such unfamiliar specimens as the tiger, the elephant, the giraffe, or the moose. And we feel a spellbound aversion for the hippopotamus, the crocodile, or the boa constrictor. To this our natural attitude toward animals a further appreciation is added when we see them acting in a photoplay. Animals are such spontaneous and natural actors, especially when contrasted with the more or less artificial human actors beside them, that part of our enjoyment in seeing them on the screen is a tribute to their reality and convincingness as ingredients in a photoplay. Furthermore, animals give us the impression of being better actors in motion pictures than in real life; and, in fact, they may be so, for the effect on the screen may be an accident or unique performance not likely to be soon repeated by the same animal. For example, a director might have to waste several hundred feet of film before he could get the policeman's horse to wink at the exact moment when his master had dismounted to flirt with a nursemaid, but the humorous effect once registered would be irresistible to the audience. Finally during all this appreciation of the animal actors we are aware of a certain irony in their position. They do not know that they are acting. They have been surprised out of their own innocence and privacy to express publicly something which they in most cases do not feel or grasp.

All this large appeal which the motion picture of nature's permanent aspects, her phenomena, and her animals holds for the spectator is a vast resource which the artist can hardly overestimate. It is not only a new medium in dramatic representation, but it is a new medium which is beautiful in itself even before it has been treated by the artist. Imagine how a painter would feel if he discovered a beautiful new colour which had never been used before in painting, or how a musician would feel if he struck a beautiful new note which had never been used before in music. The cinema composer has discovered something larger than a colour or a note. He has discovered a new domain as large as the world itself, over which he may sway the wand of art.

"The photoplay is the only art of dramatic representation which can dispense entirely with artificial settings." The dramatic advantage is that the surroundings become as real as the actors themselves. We have real people travelling over real roads in real vehicles and letting themselves in through real doors into real houses. The relation between the actor and the place of his action acquires a naturalness which could never be achieved on the stage of the spoken drama. We escape the incongruity of the stage scene where men strain themselves to tragic exhaustion in the siege of a one-sided canvas castle, or gaze rapturously off over a landscape so near that they can smell the paint of the remotest tree.

The endeavour to escape artificiality of setting is evident in the attempts of dramatic companies, amateur and professional, to perform plays out of doors, unconfined by the limits of a stage. Most of us have seen *Robin Hood* or *As You Like It* performed in some public park or on the lawn of some gentleman's estate, and have felt that there was a certain delightful appropriateness in presenting such plays beneath the blue sky and in the shadows of leaf-laden trees. There was undoubtedly a gain in charm, reality and convincingness. And yet the reality was far from complete, because the element of locomotion plays a large part in both of those plays, and that element is lacking when all of the action, from the beginning to the end of the play, is performed beneath a single clump of trees. Even when the actors in these plays are allowed to spread out to the outlying portions of their setting the environment hardly seems large enough for the diversified activities of wandering, hunting, fighting, adventuring, wooing, wedding, working, counselling, dining, playing, and resting. You may remark that the intelligent spectator can imagine that the scene has changed as often as the action needs it. But the reply is that if the spectator is to imagine that the setting has changed, he can do it more easily if the setting from which his attention changes is also an imaginary setting instead of a real one.

It is obvious that the need of keeping the audience seated in a single spot, with their attention almost continuously fixed on the play during a single session, is the condition which necessitates the localizing of action within the boundaries of a very small place, and precludes the representation of dramatic movement which occurs in going from one scene to another. If the drama were real life instead of fiction the spectator would have to follow the protagonist wherever he went, abroad and at home, indoors and out, upstairs and down. Some years ago Madame Maeterlinck tried the experiment of staging the various scenes of *Macbeth* in and about her abbey in France. Her little audience, a group of friends, wandered out a few hundred yards from the abbey to a clearing, where on one side they saw the witches in conclave, and on the other side they heard King Duncan confer a title on Macbeth. Presently they witnessed Macbeth's consternation at the witches' prophecy. Then the audience wandered back into the abbey in time to hear Lady Macbeth read the letter from her husband, who presently arrives and is encouraged to crime by the mettle of his wife. Thus the audience wandered about as the action was transferred from one portion of the environment to another. And the performance acquired a certain convincingness, despite the fact that a French abbey and the greensward of a private estate differs considerably from a Scotch castle and heath. This gain was counterbalanced, however, by the loss of emphasis (the audience in every case seeing too much of the setting), the loss of time, and the inconvenience of the audience.

The convincingness of setting and movement which the outdoor performers of stage plays have sought can be achieved by the cinematograph, which permits the spectators to sit in comfort and yet leap as quick as thought from one scene to the next, though they be hundreds of miles apart. And, although the spectators are in contact with the real environment of the action, yet the distraction of their attention is prevented, because the angle and scope of the camera limits their vision to those features of the setting which are dramatically most significant in that particular portion of the story. The cinema composer must, of course, select certain parts of the environment. That is his duty and privilege as an artist. But his selections will suggest to us dimly or subconsciously the omitted sections of his settings until in our imagination their edges touch each other and we get the feeling of a total environment. In the photoplay the physical scope of the action may be as wide as the story itself. Its action need no longer confine itself to a spot; it may spring from, or fit itself into, a complex environment. Thus for the first time in dramatic representation the spectator is permitted to remember that a single room is usually only a part of the home, that a single store-front does not make a street, nor a single street a city, that a mountain road is not a road unless you can drive over it, and that a forest is not a forest unless it is deep enough to get lost in.

In the photoplay the spectator may follow the characters and share their experiences wherever they go. Suppose that a given dramatic action consists of the siege and surrender of a mediaeval castle. We are not satisfied to be spectators from afar or from a single point of view. We wish to mingle unobserved with the furious besiegers for awhile, only to desert them for the frightened defenders within. We climb from the courtyard to the walls, where the lances are flying, and, after exposing ourselves to the enemy a few moments, we ascend to the archers in the highest tower. We return to tend the wounded in palatial apartments, we pray for victory with priests in the chapel, or we seek refuge with the frightened ladies in subterranean vaults. Thus by moving about from one spot to another and seeing both sides of the struggle in every aspect we finally realize the full significance of the action, because our experience has become more closely identified with the experience of the participants. We know now why the castle is dear to those who dwell within it, and we sympathize with the men who sacrifice their lives in its defence.

This ease of locomotion and multiplicity of setting in the photoplay is obviously a great advantage in presenting stories of action, adventure, occupation, or war. It not only enables the cinema composer to familiarize the spectator with the whole environment, but it enables him to dramatize many phases of stirring action which cannot be staged in the spoken drama. For example the tragic relation of the fugitive and the pursuer can never be realized so vividly in the drama of words as in the drama of pictures. We do not fully realize the advantage or the obstacle of distance until we travel with the characters down the road, across bridges and barriers, over land and sea, on foot or mounted, in automobile or train, in steamship, or submarine, or aeroplane. The dramatic effect of swift locomotion through natural setting was seized upon with avidity by the makers of the first motion pictures, and has been much abused in the typical and oft recurring " chase " picture. In most cases the " chase " was merely a melodramatic race of no real significance to character or story; but the stupid use of the " chase " was, of course, a fault, not of the motion picture as a medium, but of the cinema composer who had not as yet developed a sense of dramatic values in the photoplay.

Earlier in this chapter we have spoken of the absolute appeal which pure nature has for the spectator even though not used as the setting of a story. A similar absolute appeal may exist in the man-made natural setting which is in itself a work of art. The photoplay is unique among narrative arts in its capacity for utilizing and dramatizing the arts of architecture and landscape gardening. The motion picture not only brings architecture to the spectator but it gives him an appreciation of it by the method which he would employ in reality. The scene painter in the theatre can give us only one side or aspect of a cathedral. But seeing a cathedral from a single remote point of view is only one of the steps in the appreciation of the building as architecture. Having seen the cathedral from afar, a man must approach it and walk around it, he must pass beneath its portals, and wander through its aisles and transepts and chapels, he must climb its towers and peer out through its pinnacles and over its surroundings before he has come into full artistic possession of the work of the architect. The cathedral can then be appreciated, not merely as a decorative, rug-like arrangement of lines and textures, but as a handling of spaces, of distances, and heights, and depths. The man may measure it with his own stature as the measuring rod. He may feel it above and beneath and around himself.

Let it not be supposed that we consider it a function

From the Lasky *Carmen.* Four locales, the foreground, the courtyard, the dark archway, and the country beyond, are presented simultaneously, yet unity of pictorial composition is preserved by the principle of perspective. See page 43.

of the photoplay to educate the spectator in the appreciation of architecture. We have in mind merely the subordinate use of natural setting in the service of the dramatic action. The materials of the cinema composer must be given integral value in his finished work. No single light must be allowed to eclipse the whole creation. Just as the spoken drama sometimes may dramatize a song, as in *Trilby*, or an aesthetic dance, as in *The Doll's House*, so the photoplay may sometimes dramatize the visual beauty of architecture or of landscape gardening. If the song or the dance is merely an interpolation which might easily be omitted, the playwright is guilty of bad construction. If the bit of architecture or the beautiful garden is merely a detachable decoration the cinema composer has revealed his ignorance of artistic unity. For example, the artificial and formal elegance of a garden should be utilized only when it harmonizes with the artificial and formal elegance of the characters in that environment. The delicate luxury of the conservatory may well be used as a background for the girl who is herself a hot-house plant.

It may occur to some critical person that natural settings are often imitated, or " faked " by the producer, and that therefore we are talking in vain. There are two replies to the critic. The first is that we are talking of the highest possibilities, not of the commonest usage. We are pointing out what the producer might do if he wanted to declare dividends in art instead of in cash. The second reply is that in the photoplay, curiously enough, the perfectly imitated setting is to all intents and purposes just as real as the real setting. The caravan travelling over the sandy wastes of California may take on all the reality of the caravan in the Desert of Sahara. Sand is sand, and camels are camels, and actors who act well lose their given names, their surnames, their identities and become the characters of the play. In interiors especially, the imitation, if at all well done, may be as good as the genuine article. If the average spectator cannot tell the difference between the scene actually photographed in " The Little Church Around the Corner " and the imitated scene photographed in the motion picture studio, there is certainly no point in disillusioning him. Convincingness, no matter how acquired, is the desired quality in any art. And it is only because in many cases the natural setting and real nature are so much more convincing than the imitated setting that we grow enthusiastic over their use in the photoplay.

Up to this point we have been discussing nature and natural setting as rich, new material for the cinema composer. We have emphasized the irresistible appeal to the eye of the spectator which exists in every phase of nature as unmodified by man. We have alluded to the photoplaywright's opportunity of utilizing the natural setting which is itself an art product of man. We have shown that deep reality and convincingness results when a setting is used as an environment instead of a mere background for the action. Now that we have examined the nature of these new materials, let us see how the cinema composer may use them in a photoplay.

The proper use of the setting is a great responsibility which no photoplaywright can shirk. The novelist may ignore his settings for page after page, and the reader, of course, forgets all about them. But in the photoplay the setting is always there before the eye of the spectator, whether it concerns the action or not.   He cannot escape it; he must look at it.   Therefore it is of vital importance that the setting, not only does not distract the attention of the spectator, but that it actually reinforce the dramatic value of the action.   The intensifying of a situation by placing it in an appropriate setting can be done much more vividly in the photoplay than in the novel, because in the photoplay the setting can be presented simultaneously with the action, while in the novel, since no two words or sentences can occupy the same place at the same time, the description of the setting must either precede or follow the description of the action.

The cinema composer may handle his setting in five different ways.   He may have a *neutral* setting, one which neither hinders nor helps the action.   He may make the setting *informative;* that is, he may let the setting convey some element of the story which is not conveyed in any other way.   The setting may be *sympathetic,* or harmonizing with the general mood or impression of the action.   The setting may be *participating;* that is, it may enter integrally into the action of the story.   And the setting may be *formative;* that is, it may actually exercise some power in moulding the characters in the play.

The neutral setting is much desired by the producer because it enables him to stage the play cheaply and haphazardly in the sets which are most easily built in his studio, and in the " locations " where his company happens to be working at the time.   There can be no objection to the neutral setting if it really is neutral, if it really gets no attention whatsoever from the spec-

tator.   It is all very well to have a duel take place
somewhere out among the trees, providing the trees
are not evergreens trimmed into fantastic shapes, for
in such case the spectator would contemplate the trees
rather than the duelists.   It is not objectionable for a
diplomat and a spy to be shown meeting in a restaurant, providing the other diners are not more interesting to our eyes than the diplomat and the spy.   If a
given story can be staged as effectively in the moun-
tains as at the sea shore, there is obviously no vital
connection between the story and the setting.   It is
merely the duty of the director to see to it that neither
the rocks nor the surf get more attention than the
action of the story.   But judging by the films which
we see in most of the motion picture theatres it is
evident that the majority of directors are notoriously
blind to the actual significance of a setting.   While
the scenario writer is waiting for these busy men to
mature into artists, he must guard his scenario carefully.   If he chooses an arbitrary setting in order to
make his story more saleable, let him choose one which
is not likely to become unneutral in careless hands.

Many of the directors are already trying to vital-
ize the setting, to give it a definite share in producing
the total artistic effect of the photoplay.   When the
scenario writer can hope to impress, if not to educate,
such men, and can look forward confidently to their
intelligent interpretation of his composition, he is
bound as an artist to dramatize his setting.   The least
that he can demand of his setting is that it be informative, that is, either descriptive or narrative.   For
example, a character may be described by the environment which he has himself created.   A single glance

about the room of a man whom we have never seen may tell us more about his character and identity than a whole page of description. If you see five or six college pennants on the wall, a poster of a chorus girl, a sign board with the legend "Family Entrance" or "No Dumping Here," two or three beer steins and the picture of a man in football togs on the mantelpiece, a book case with seven or eight books on the top shelf, a stack of magazines on the next, and a pair of dancing pumps on the bottom shelf, a desk groaning beneath tobacco jars, pipes, and a mandolin, you may safely guess that the occupant is, or has recently been, a certain type of college freshman. His room describes him, and your acquaintance with him begins even before he himself appears. Now let us suppose that the freshman is a character in a play, the other characters being the freshman's father (a tired business man of New York), the professor of Greek, a chorus girl, and a boarding house keeper. Each one of these characters could be introduced in his or her own typical surroundings, surroundings which were silent but eloquent descriptions of the characters introduced. In the stage play these same characters would be vividly revealed by their manner of speech and the words they used." In the cinema play there is no legitimate description except through physical appearances, shape, mien, attitude, gesture, act, and, as we have just shown, physical environment. And if words must be dispensed with, all the other means of expression must be mobilized and energized.

In the use of descriptive setting the photoplay can be superior to the stage play because it is subject neither to place nor time. Where the stage play might describe the environment of one character, the photoplay could present the environments of twenty, and in less time than it takes to change from one stage set to another.   Or it could present twenty different aspects of the environment of a single character, or of a class of people in a certain social level.   Thus, while Hauptmann in his stage drama of the rebellious weavers must limit himself to three or four settings, all of them interiors, the photoplay could present the same group indoors and out, at their looms, and at their humble amusements, gossiping in their tiny dooryards, driving bargains in the village market place or in narrow shops, drinking in dark taverns, trying in vain to make happy homes out of dingy hovels, and organizing mobs in front of their employers' palaces.   In Hauptmann's play it is the crowd or community as a whole, rather than any individual, which is dramatized.   But dialog alone cannot give us a complete insight into the psychology of the community of weavers.   We must see for ourselves the physical conditions under which they live and work.   We, too, must come in contact with their surroundings if we would completely understand their feelings.   Their environment must reveal to our eyes the facts which we could never grasp in words.   Such information and such impressions the photoplay can give by dramatizing the setting itself and giving it a descriptive power in the play.

It would even be possible to let a setting tell part of the story, to stimulate our imagination by informing us of happenings in the immediate past.   A good example of narrative setting was seen in Winchell Smith's stage play *The Fortune Hunter* in which John Barrymore appeared a few seasons ago.   The

play relates the story of Duncan, a city youth out of
funds, who is advised to seek his fortune in some
country village.   Duncan gets a position in a drug store.
We see him behind a shabby counter, before poverty
stricken shelves bearing only a few dust covered bottles, and amidst equipment that is mutely complaining
of failing business.   We have just begun to wonder
what fortune Duncan can find here, when the curtain
drops.   When it rises on the next act one swift glance
of the eye reveals a new soda fountain of finest marble
and plate glass mirrors, lavishly equipped with up-to-
the-minute devices for mixing soft drinks, a pharmis-
try with trim shelves and endless rows of neatly or-
dered bottles, and counters and show cases that seem
animate with prosperity.   No characters need tell us
in words what has happened.   The whole setting is
itself narrative.   In a flash it relates the story of prosperity.   This single example of a descriptive setting
becoming narrative should help the cinema composer
to recall or invent other situations where physical
environment is dramatized and forced into active service in the story.

"We cannot emphasize too strongly the principle that
in an art where the appeal is entirely through the eye
alone it is important that everything the eye sees should
reinforce, or harmonize with, the impression which the
story endeavours to make." No piece of art, whether
it be a cathedral, a symphony, a painting, a poem, a
statue, a prose fiction, or a photoplay can ever be
looked upon as perfect unless it has the unity which
results from a complete harmony of all its parts.   In
the photoplay the setting, an ever present, ever visible
part, can sometimes be made interpretative of, or sym-

pathetic with, the characters or action of the play, thus harmonizing with the matter and meaning of the whole. In the handling of sympathetic setting the cinema composer has much to learn from the masters of literature. Observe Poe in *The Fall of the House of Usher* fusing setting and action together with consummate art until they convey a single irresistible impression. His first sentence sets the key. " During the whole of a dull, dark, and soundless day in the autumn of the year, when the clouds hung oppressively low in the heavens, I had been passing alone, on horseback, through a singularly dreary tract of country; and at length found myself, as the shades of the evening drew on, within view of the melancholy House of Usher. . . . I looked upon the scene before me . . . upon the mere house, and the simple landscape features of the domain . . . upon the bleak walls . . . upon the vacant eye-like windows . . . upon a few rank sedges . . . and upon a few white trunks of decayed trees . . . with an utter depression of soul . . ." The author then goes on to describe the house itself, ending with these lines: " Beyond this indication of extensive decay, however, the fabric gave little token of instability. Perhaps the eye of a scrutinizing observer might have discovered a barely perceptible fissure, which, extending from the roof of the building in front, made its way down the wall in a zigzag direction, until it became lost in the sullen waters of the tarn." Every detail of the setting helps to create the mood of gloom and impending doom, which is maintained throughout the tale until the gruesome, agonizing death of Roderick Usher.

Another example of sympathetic setting is to be

From *Audrey*. An excellent example of sympathetic setting as well as of harmony in the composition of lines. The vertical, without being obtrusive, are everywhere present — in the architecture, in the hanging moss, and in the costumes and poses of the figures. These physical values are in sympathy with the emotion of the characters. See page 186.

found in Hugo's *Notre Dame de Paris*.   In this novel the mysterious and magnificent Gothic cathedral harmonizes with the mood of the story.   The hunchback Quasimodo is like a gargoyle come to life, and the white-robed Esmeralda is like a reincarnation of a figure from an altarpiece.   Around the cathedral surge the superstitious, fickle, motley-minded crowds of Paris, glimpsing an ideal here and there, and destined to rise into noble nationality, just as the cathedral itself rises from the chaos of rough materials through the apparent disorder of building into a thing of aspiring stability and beauty.

In stage drama, too, the sympathetic setting is often effectively used. Ibsen's *Ghosts* begins amid the gloom of a grey day and the damp bleakness of a Norwegian fjord, continues through the hectic glow of the burning orphanage, and ends with tragic irony in the bright dawn of a fair day.   Throughout the play the setting helps to interpret the philosophic progress of a community which through tragic experience frees itself from dead ideals and outworn conventions and marches into the bright day of social happiness.

To make the setting reinforce the impression of the story is even more important in the cinema play than in fiction or spoken drama.   And it can easily be done if the director is provided with an artistically composed scenario and is disposed to translate it faithfully to the screen.   He must exercise extreme care in supervising the designing and building of artificial sets, and must have a keen eye for the interpreting power of nature and natural setting.   If an additional outlay of money is necessary for the successful harmonizing of action with setting it will surely be forthcoming when the producer discovers that a piece of art, like a machine, in which every part functions is more economical and has more enduring value than one in which half of the material is dead weight. But the value of a photoplay may often be increased without increasing its cost. The world is full of expressive settings waiting to be harmonized with some action, and the director should not neglect any opportunity for improving even a single scene in a play. Thus two men of brute instincts fighting in a primitive way would be composed into a better picture if shown beneath the scraggly branch of a gnarled old oak, than if shown on the front porch of a house. For the society girl of a certain type the sparkling fountain would be a suitable complement. The poet-dreamer should walk beneath the aspiring poplars, and not beneath the apple trees. The lonely recluse should build his hut on the edge of the desert. The inventor should work amidst a maze of machinery. The gambler should revel in the atmosphere of Monte Carlo. The lovers should plight their troth beneath blossoming trees. The veteran soldier should be seated in the park near an antiquated cannon. The grandmother should be shown gazing off over harvested fields. We do not mean that the action of a play should ever be distorted in order to produce such effects, but we do insist that the significance of many a scene or character could often be emphasized in some such manner as we have indicated.

Total impression and meaning of a play as a whole may often be deepened by dramatizing nature herself. A good example is the Blue Bird photoplay *Undine,* an adaptation of Fouqué's fairy story. Undine, child of the waves, is literally born of the sea. She is a pagan personification of inanimate nature, and differs from the other characters in the story in that she has no soul, and can get one only by marrying a mortal. It can be seen at once that to make this story effective, two things must be emphasized, the sea and the element of the supernatural. This the photoplay does. We are ever kept in the presence of the sea, the surf, wild beaches, damp caves, shelving shores, sea weed, mermaids, and marine monsters. This gives us the right mood and helps us to believe that Undine is literally a child of the waves. The supernatural, too, is emphasized by means of camera magic. For this we are taken into the dark, mysterious forest, where waterfalls turn into giants, where wood nymphs materialize and vanish amid drooping vines, where dwarfs spring out of the ground in our pathway. Always the setting hypnotizes us and weaves about us the spell of illusion until we never doubt this fairy story which we know could not possibly be true.

If we contrast this harmony of action and environment in *Undine* with the haphazard use of marine setting in the Lasky *Carmen* we see at once the difference between art and mere carpentry. *Carmen* opens with a beautiful picture of the sea and high wooded banks. In the foreground a man is silhouetted against the bright sea and sky. That is the key to the action. But it is the wrong key, because *Carmen* is in no sense a marine play. The picture is bad because it puts us in the wrong mood, and because it is so striking that it is hard to forget it, and get into the right mood.

Earlier in this chapter we have spoken of the cinematic value of animals. We tried to explain just why audiences liked to see them on the screen. But it is not enough for the cinema composer that animals are merely interesting to the audience. He should endeavour to make the dumb brutes communicative as well as interesting. Even when they are introduced as part of the environment, rather than as actors in a story, they may be given a symbolic value and may become part of the sympathetic setting. For example, the dog may be made something more than a pet. He may be on the screen what he has been for thousands of years in literature and art, the animate symbol of faithfulness. Many an abstract idea can thus be concretely expressed in the form of an animal. The innocent kitten, or lamb, the hen mothering her brood, the blustering cock, the vain peacock, the cooing turtledove, the awkward calf, the wise owl, the regal lion, the fleet deer, the graceful gazelle, the clever fox, the humorous monkey, the satanic serpent — all can be so dramatized that they harmonize with and reinforce the mood or meaning in any particular scene in a cinema play.

As to the method of handling sympathetic setting we may say what we have already said about symbolism. The expressiveness of mere things should be subordinated to the expressiveness of human beings. The emphasis should always be on character, and the environment should be an echo rather than a note. It is not even necessary that the spectator be aware of the interpretative value of the setting. The subconscious influence is sometimes more potent than the conscious. And it is in this subconscious appeal, the appeal which the spectator cannot understand, that he feels the magic and divinity of art.

Sometimes a natural setting may be given a participating function, an acting part in the drama. In Bulwer-Lytton's *Last Days of Pompeii,* for example, the plot is resolved by the eruption of Vesuvius. After many murmurs and threats the volcano comes like an angry god to lower the curtain of death upon the human drama. In Bret Harte's *The Luck of Roaring Camp* another natural phenomenon ends the humorously pathetic story of the miner and the orphaned, illegitimate baby. A mountain flood blots out the camp. The miner attempts to rescue the infant " and the strong man, clinging to the frail babe as a drowning man is said to cling to a straw, drifted away into the shadowy river that flows for ever to the unknown sea." Here we note a touch of symbolism in the natural phenomenon which participates with such climactic force in the action. In another of the same author's stories, *The Outcasts of Poker Flat,* nature participates in the climax of the action, again with symbolic effect. The snow storm ends the career of the outcasts, who are too bad to dwell even in the liberal community of Poker Flat. A drunkard, a gambler, a prostitute, and a keeper of a disorderly resort are driven out of the village. They travel into the foot hills, and when they make camp for the night they are accidentally joined by a pair of innocent and pure-minded lovers. During the night a snow storm arises. The party is snow bound, and within the next few days all except one die from starvation and cold. Our attention is especially fixed on the prostitute and the innocent girl. " Feathery drifts of snow, shaken from the long pine-boughs, flew like white-winged birds, and settled about them as they slept. The moon through the rifted clouds looked down upon what had been the camp. But all human stain, all trace of earthly travail, was hidden beneath the spotless mantle mercifully flung from above. . . . And when pitying fingers brushed the snow from their wan faces, you could scarcely have told from the equal peace that dwelt upon them, which was she that had sinned."

Such organization of natural phenomena into plots has hitherto been permitted to literature alone. "The stage play has never been able to utilize floods, rapids, typhoons, avalanches, icebergs, and volcanic eruptions except with the most artificial and unconvincing results." The representation of avenging thunderbolts, snow storms, and sand storms has been attempted on the stage, but the effects have too often been enveloped in melodrama. This points us to the danger facing the cinema composer who wishes to make nature a participating factor in his story. He must beware lest the phenomenon become merely a crude spectacle, a flagrant "punch," entirely out of key with the rest of the action.

There is still another way of dramatizing nature and natural setting. It is to reveal the slow but certain work of physical environment in altering and moulding human character. While character is the cause of action, the setting may sometimes be dramatized as the cause of character. Formative setting has been described in fiction and it can be represented in the motion pictures, because the camera can go anywhere and can bring to the attention of the spectators everything which the dramatic character would see, and be influenced by, in real life. It can range from the entire sky line of a great city to the numerals on the ticker tape, from the vast loneliness of the desert to the tiny prickles of the cactus, from the endless surge of the ocean to the age-worn pebble on the beach.   It can select and emphasize and insistently repeat those features and details of physical environment which would in the course of months and years enter into the souls of the characters within that environment.

Again the cinema composer may learn his lesson from the practice of fiction writers.   Thomas Hardy in *The Return of the Native* and in *Tess of the D'Urbervilles* represents his characters as literally children of the soil.   Even prenatally they have been infused with the utter gloom and dreariness of the moors. They are hard and pessimistic and drifting toward tragedy, because nature about them is barren and unpromising and unconsoling.   Hardy with his mastery of words can make the reader see clearly and feel vividly the broad aspects as well as the minutest detail of this formative setting.   He makes him understand its irresistible influence in the development of human character.   Another illustration of the formative power of nature is John Masefield's narrative poem " Dauber " in *The Story of a Round House.* The hero, an English farmer boy, desirous of becoming a marine painter, ships as a common sailor on a vessel bound for Valparaiso.   During the first few days of the voyage he is naturally looked upon as a land lubber, and because he paints, and paints badly, is dubbed " The Dauber " by his ship mates.   But the call of the sea and the call of art are louder than the voices of mockers.   The farmer boy scrubs the deck, and stands by the tackle, and goes up to the mast head until he becomes an able seaman. And always, beneath the sun of the equator, the starlight of the Southern cross, and through the storms off Cape Horn, he gazes steadily upon his companions, upon the ship, upon wave and horizon and cloud, until he penetrates the mysterious truths of the sailor's soul and the sailor's sea. But he is himself a product of all that he has looked upon. And as we read the sounding cadences of Masefield's verse we see in imagination the powerful processes by which nature produces a character.

We have given these literary masterpieces as illustrations of method rather than of material. Perhaps the formative settings of Hardy and Masefield could not adequately be represented in motion pictures. Then let the photoplay beat a new path by applying old methods to new material. Scenario editors complain that the most hackneyed and oft recurring plot is the story of the innocent girl or boy who comes from the country to the city and becomes the victim of new surroundings. Why should these scenarios always be rejected? Perhaps because the writers who have looked upon the city as a formative setting have undertaken to energize it in words instead of in pictures. If we in the audience are to understand the effect of the city upon the unsophisticated girl we must see what she sees, we must go where she goes. Her face is not expressive to us unless we also see the physical things upon which her gaze is directed. We must see with her the labyrinthine streets and byways, the busy maze of haggling customers and shop keepers, skyscrapers towering into the clouds and casting their shadows upon hovels, the apparent chaos of streets and bridges, the endless weaving of water traffic, art museums and gambling dens, cathedrals and night courts, excursion steamers and dance halls, the curb market and the midnight cabaret, the flood of limousines on Fifth Avenue and the homegoing subway throngs more tightly packed than war prisoners. All these things and more must be shown to us in the special aspects which the story demands, until we begin to feel what the dramatic character feels, and can sympathize with her if she is overwhelmed or confused or misled or crushed, a victim of her surroundings.

Whoever can cinematize this theme successfully, or can find other, better themes and treat them freshly and forcefully by making the setting itself formative in the manner we have suggested will make a distinct contribution to the progress of the art of the cinema play. Whoever will come with courage, philosophy, and imagination to the problems of dramatizing the setting, of applying in screen practice these theories of neutral, informative, sympathetic, participating, and formative settings may do for the photoplay as much service as Gordon Craig, Max Reinhardt, and Granville Barker have done for the stage play. If it was necessary for the spoken drama that the setting should be made an important part rather than an accessory, then it is much more important for the drama of silent pictures that the silence shall be vocalized, and mute, inanimate things be endowed with a living language.

CHAPTER IX

WORDS ON THE SCREEN

NATURE abhors a mixture of species and therefore does not allow hybrid animals to perpetuate themselves by reproduction. The history of the development of aesthetic taste shows the same abhorrence for hybrid art. Hybrid art is not pure and therefore cannot endure as art. Some of the Greeks, for example, tried the cross-breeding of arts by painting complexions on their statues, but the resulting hybrid, half painting and half sculpture, could not endure as art and is remembered in history only as an interesting mistake. The great masterpieces of sculpture, as of any other art, represent the development of that art in its purest form. The photoplay as an art form consists of a composition of pictured motions. And since words are neither pictures nor motions they would seem to have no place in the photoplay. Yet no cinema composer has ever had the courage or the genius to produce a photoplay of any length which accomplished its artistic purpose entirely without the aid of words on the screen. In fact, the photoplays we see are so full of words that we must spend one third, or even half, of our time reading words, and the remainder of the time appreciating pictures. And our interests are so divided that we are impressed neither by the literature nor by the pictures.

Yet we would not be so radical as to say that words

may never be admitted to a photoplay. In the first place it may be said that words do not spoil the purity of a picture play if they are really an organic part of the picture, that is, if they are really in the subject which is photographed. Suppose, for example, that we have as a given setting a hallway with an office door bearing the legend, " John Anderson, Attorney-at-Law." A gentleman comes into the picture, opens the door, and shows by his action in the following picture that he is in his own office. Those words are dramatically important because they identify the hero, and are artistically admissible because they belong organically in the picture. Or suppose that a prodigal son runs away from his rather comfortable looking home to seek adventure in far away lands. He does not write to his parents, who finally give him up as lost forever. But after years have passed the son decides to return and ask forgiveness. As he hurries along the street he sees from a distance that his old home is in a rather rundown condition, and as he turns in at the front gate he sees in the window a sign " To Let " and realizes that repentance has come too late. Those words are dramatic and are in no way pictorially out of harmony. Both of these cases illustrate the use of organic words in a photoplay, but the name on the door, being merely a device for identification, is less commendable than the sign in the window, which institutes sharply a dramatic situation.

Now it must be remembered that the moment we approve of organic words in the motion picture we are exposing the cinema composer to the temptation to express more things in words than in the pantomime or motion picture proper. He will proceed through

"Lost or Strayed" signs, epitaphs on tombstones, and "Rewards for Capture" to "Mayor's Proclamations" two or three hundred words in length until he is actually presenting his story in words accompanied by pictures as comments on the words.   How far then shall the composer be allowed to go in his reliance on words as first aids to the silent play of people, things, and places in motion?   We should say that as a general principle words should be admitted to the photoplay only when they intensify the dramatic value of the particular picture of which they are a part, or when they express indispensable things which could not possibly be expressed in any other cinematic way.

It is, of course, obvious that no combination of trees, houses, or facial expressions could ever tell an audience that a man's name was Jack Robinson.   A name is a word, and as a word it must appear in the photoplay.   This may be on a visiting card, shown in a close-up, or on an addressed envelope, or as a signature at the bottom of a letter or a document, or it may appear in dozens of other ways, all of which may be looked upon as necessary and permissible devices for identifying characters.   But the true artist can make a virtue of necessity, can dramatize a device. Once the word has been introduced it may reappear at the psychological moment with dramatic effect. Thus the wife may be confronted with her husband's signature to a treasonable document, or the husband may be shocked to find his wife's name at the end of an incriminating letter to some notorious man.   The word has become a dramatized organic part of the picture.

Letters, documents, telegrams, newspaper clippings,

book pages, etc., may all be looked upon as organic words. In fact, letters and telegrams produce some of the most dramatic moments in our lives. Such devices have been effectively used throughout the whole period of stage drama. And they may be used still more effectively on the screen. Written communications are meant to be read with the eyes and not with the lips. Lady Macbeth, though all alone on the stage, must read aloud the letter which she has just received from her husband. Bob Acres, struggling with the composition of his famous challenge, must repeat aloud the sentences which he scratches down on paper. If these letters were not read aloud the audience would, of course, never discover their contents. But in the case of the photoplay the letters, being presented to the spectators' eyes and not to their ears, make the experience of the spectators coincide more exactly with the experience of the characters. In fact, an actor may extend his interpretation of a part even to the handwriting of the character, and this visual interpretation may appear in the letter which is shown on the screen.

While the true artist may dramatize an expedient, the bungling hack will surely abuse it. He will resort frequently to the letter or other communication on the screen until the entire plot of his play is projected in words and would be equally clear and equally impressive with or without the accompanying pictures. Such a composition is no photoplay; it is simply an illustrated novel which the spectators are forced to read simultaneously, all turning pages at the same instant. In order to transform such a composition into a proper photoplay one would first of all have to make the pictures paramount in expressiveness. Then one would have to apply the principles of probability and verisimilitude to the literary devices. Letters and telegrams should be sent only under the circumstances when they would normally be sent in real life. And they should, of course, contain only the information and expression which a person would ordinarily communicate in such a way. Likewise newspaper headlines, "want ads," and "personals" and all similar reading matter should appear in the photoplay for the edification of the audience only when they are probable, organic, dramatic parts of the life portrayed on the screen.

Another class of reading matter for the cinema audience is formed by the extraneous words of the photoplay, words which are entirely outside the pictures, words of whose existence no character in the plot is aware. The cinematic effectiveness of such interpolations, which may be generally termed "subtitles," depends on their content, length, and frequency.

First of all we must observe that the sub-title, not being an organic part of the story, interrupts and arrests the story. This interruption is excusable if it carries the plot over some omitted period of time or directs the spectator's attention to some necessary action which could not properly be cinematized, and it is desirable if it increases the pictorial or dramatic beauty of the pictures. But in any case it is an interruption. The author stops his tale for a while, and communicates directly with his audience, explaining or commenting upon his plot. To be sure, instead of actually saying, "Now, ladies and gentle-

men, let us assume that one year has passed," he
merely projects on the screen the words "A Year
Later." The audience reads this in three seconds,
one second being allowed for each word on the screen,
and mentally adjust themselves to the plausible consequences of the lapse of time. Had the sub-title read
"A Century Later" the mental leap must have been
made with the same alacrity. It will be seen at once
that if the author becomes too highly selective of
periods of time for his action he will force the audience to make too many new adjustments of mind, and
will forestall all possibility of unified continuous attention. The cinema composer should make a careful comparison between his devices for indicating lapse
of time and the devices used in the stage play. In the
stage play the curtain is dropped, and the program
informs us how much of a recess we are to have,
whether one minute or twelve, also how much time is
supposed to have elapsed when the curtain next rises.
Sometimes the dialog at the beginning of the next scene
defines the length of the dramatic interval which separates that scene from the previous one. All this
machinery, though it may seem cumbersome, really
is psychologically effective, and makes the audience
feel that the indicated interval of time really has
elapsed. To make the sub-title psychologically effective is the concern of the scenario writer. Miss
Anita Loos, a skilful title writer for the Douglas
Fairbanks plays, has suggested that a short lapse of
time should be indicated by a brief sub-title, and
a long lapse by a long sub-title. Such reasoning is in
the right direction. But perhaps best of all is to re-
duce the cinematic lapses of time to a minimum. If

a two hour stage play uses two lapses of time, how many should a one hour photoplay use? Certainly not one every ten minutes.

The sub-title must sometimes be used to allude to dramatic action which cannot be presented on the screen either because it is mechanically impossible to do so or because propriety forbids. Similar omitted actions in the case of the stage play may, of course, be alluded to in the conversation of the characters. And the conversation itself may be so minimized and manipulated that a vast amount of information reaches the audience through the pauses, intonations, and facial expression of the actor. But no such allusiveness is possible on the screen. Whatever the word or phrase is, it stands out uncompromising and unsubdued, sharply isolated between two pictures. The scenario writer must, therefore, exercise the greatest care when he is forced to resort to words as aids to his true medium of motion pictures.

"The most desirable of all auxiliary words in the photoplay are those which really intensify the beauty of the picture they accompany." Often a picture gains in value if it is interpreted or if the audience is put in the right psychological mood for it. Even painters sometimes use words to convey something which is not conveyed by paint. For example, Breton has a painting of a peasant girl with a sickle in her hand. She is gazing upward with rapt attention. Behind her on the horizon is the half orb of the sun. But the picture does not take on its full meaning until we read the title, "The Song of the Lark." Then our auditory imagination is appealed to; we hear the unseen lark and feel the emotions of the peasant girl.

Similarly, Millet's " The Angelus " (Vesper Bells) would not convey its full meaning without the words in the title. The photoplay may use the sub-title with similar effect. The sub-title may further enrich a picture by interpreting it or by putting the audience in suspense for it. In this function the sub-title of a photoplay bears a strong resemblance to the chapter heading of a novel. Walter Scott, for example, almost invariably struck the key of a chapter by prefacing it with a quotation from poetry. Thus in *Ivanhoe* the chapters dealing chiefly with Isaac or Rebecca are prefaced with a few lines from *The Merchant of Venice* or from *The Jew of Malta,* and the chapters describing battles are introduced with appropriate lines from Shakespeare's historical plays. George Eliot in *Romola* arouses the reader's suspense by the chapter headings " A Face in the Crowd," " Tito's Dilemma," and " The Garment of Fear." Suspense is aroused more obviously in Bulwer-Lytton's *The Last Days of Pompeii* by such headings as " The Stream of Love Runs on — Whither? " and " A Wasp Ventures into the Spider's Web." In all these cases the chapters are read more eagerly and remembered more vividly because of the author's interruptions which precede them. But the analogy between subtitles and chapter headings must not be pushed too far. The chapters of a novel are logical divisions which have no corresponding parts in the photoplay. Besides, the number of words in chapter headings is very small when compared with the number in the entire novel. Even in the most exaggerated cases, as for example in *Ivanhoe,* the verses which head the chapters constitute only one percent. of the total num-

ber of words. At that rate a one hour photoplay
would be allowed only thirty-six words for sub-titles,
and according to the proportion in *The Last Days
of Pompeii* the same photoplay would be allowed only
twelve words, this on the assumption that one word
be allowed per second of projection.

"In the case of comedy the author may often very
effectively interrupt his dramatic action for the sake
of making a humorous comment upon it." For example, a devout faced husband bids his disappointed
wife good night immediately after dinner on the plea
that he must visit a sick friend. We see him go out;
then comes a sub-title " His Sick Friend "; and the
following picture shows our kindhearted philanthro-
pist with four or five husky men playing poker around
a bottle-laden table. The spectator would, of course,
have been amused at the husband's lie even without
the sub-title; but the author's ironical comment sharp-
ens the humour of the situation.

These interpolated comments of the composer himself, though opposite in tone, are somewhat in the
manner of the chorus in Greek tragedy, which makes
a running comment on the play. Contemporary playwrights have in many instances substituted for the
spoken comments of the chorus a type of humorous
stage direction within parentheses. These parenthet-
ical remarks, of course, play no part in a stage performance, since there is no one to speak them, but are
much relished by readers of the printed plays. Thus
Barrie interpolates the following comment on his
hero in *Rosalind:* " young man . . . modest and clear-
eyed and would ring for his tub in Paradise . . .
To him the proper way to look upon ability is as

something we must all come to in the end." And
Bernard Shaw in describing the stage setting for the
first scene in *Cæsar and Cleopatra* says inconsequen-
tially " The stars and the cloudless sky are our own
contemporaries, nineteen and a half centuries younger
than we know them; but you would not guess that
from their appearance."

Interpolations in the photoplay have already reached
the point where an author jests at his own expense,
or, in the parlance of the studio, " kids the film along."
This habit of jesting at one's own tale was common
among the novelists a century and a half ago.   Field-
ing, for example, in *Tom Jones* invariably makes such
light hearted remarks as the following about the story
he tells: " Book III, Chapter I.   Containing little or
nothing "; Book VII, Chapter X.   Containing several
matters, natural enough perhaps, but low "; " Book
XI, Chapter III.   A very short chapter, in which however is a sun, a moon, a star, and an angel."

Thus sub-titles may be used in the photoplay for
humorous effect or to prepare the audience psychologically for the dramatic value in the following pictures.
All such sub-titles are very well in their place, but
their place is a small one.   A photoplay is a single
progression of pictures, but this progression will be
neither single nor direct if the author makes his by-
paths as broad, as deep, and as long as the main
thoroughfare.   After all the play's the thing, and
by-plays are only thingumbobs.

A third class of words on the screen is the projection of printed dramatic dialog.   Screen dialog differs
from the organic words in photoplay letters, signs, etc.,
because it is not pictorially a part of the play, and it

differs from the sub-title because it is dramatically in the play and not in the author's comments on the play. "Screen dialog can never be as effective as stage dialog, which gains its force by being spoken." Besides screen dialog never really accompanies the action. It does not even synchronize with the character's dialog, coming as it does, either a few seconds too soon or too late for his lip movement and facial expression. Yet scenario writers, under the wild illusion that they are competing with playwrights, insist on cutting in or fading in dialog which their characters are supposed to speak. They may retort that stage plays are sometimes printed and that dramatic dialog may be very impressive to a reader; but the reply to that is that the reader of a printed play is not interrupted at the end of every seven or eight words and forced to look at a picture on the opposite page before he can continue with the rest of the speech. Dramatic dialog to be impressive must either be read continuously or heard continuously, otherwise the spell will be broken. Since neither one of these conditions can be satisfied in the motion pictures, we recommend that photoplay dialog be left entirely to inference or to the imagination. Just how this may be done we have already shown in the chapter on " Imagination." The cinema composer who strives to present dialog by inference and through the imagination of the audience is a true artist, because he is endeavouring to energize one of the supposed limitations of his medium.

Taking advantage of a limitation is no less important than discovering and exploiting new possibilities of a medium. And the motion pictures present a number of interesting possibilities in the manipulation of words. For example, by a strange effect of camera magic, words may be represented as literally darting through the air. In the Famous Players' version of *The Poor Little Rich Girl* is a scene in which the governess locks the little heroine in a room. The girl gets revenge by hissing through the key-hole " I hate you, I hate you! ", the seething words actually shooting through the key-hole in the direction of the outraged governess. That words are physical things palpable to the eye is a pleasing fancy and the whimsical proof on the screen constitutes a new pictorial appeal. Another unique treatment of words is effected by the camera device of dissolving one word or line of words into another word or line. For example, a letter in some foreign language may be shown on the screen, and the moment the audience starts puzzling over it the writing dissolves into words of our own language, the letter, so to speak, translating itself before our eyes. Or a secret communication may be shown in cipher code and the decoding may take place in the same easy manner. We may even in time develop a cinema punster, a wit who presents one of his double meanings in a sub-title and the other a moment later not in a word but in a picture.

From all that has been said it must be clear that we look upon words as subordinate, rather than as co-ordinate, parts of a cinematic composition. But even when introduced as mere auxiliaries screen words may accomplish a vast amount of harm in a photoplay. An interpolated sub-title or a screened letter may violate all the principles of pictorial composition which the cinematic artist is trying to apply. Composition in static and fluent forms involves, of course, the composition of all the visible values which appear on the screen.   Hence the so-called title editor of a studio should be no less a composer of pictures than the man who designs the setting or directs the action.   Commendable attempts are already being made to preserve pictorial harmony by decorating sub-titles with charcoal or wash drawings or by interweaving the words with photographic pictures.   In discussing symbolism we showed how decorated sub-titles might be used for symbolic effect, but here we are concerned with the preservation of pictorial unity, emphasis, balance, and rhythm.   For example, in a picture play laid in a western setting marginal etchings of saddles, lariats, pistols, cactus, sage brush, etc., may preserve the continuity of the tonal and line values of the pictorial composition as well as keep the audience in the mood of the story.   But even when no such auxiliary decoration is resorted to, much can be accomplished by keeping the style of the lettering and the background of the words in artistic harmony with the pictorial series.

But however and whenever words are used in the photoplay it must be remembered that a photoplay is first and last a picture play, and that whenever non-pictorial devices are introduced they must be introduced for the betterment of that picture play.   As one jarring note may spoil a piece of music so one unsightly moment may vitiate the fluent beauty of a cinematic composition.

CHAPTER X

THOMAS NAST became famous as a caricaturist because he amused millions of readers of newspapers and magazines, helped the North win the Civil War by his sketches, and introduced many of the humorous symbols and methods of the modern school of political cartoonists. Frans Hals immortalized himself among painters by putting character and individuality into his pleasing portraits of laughing men and women of Seventeenth Century Holland. Aristophanes, Plautus, Terence, Molière, Ben Jonson, Sheridan, Gilbert, Shaw, and Barrie are great names in the history of stage comedy. What composer of screen comedy will become equally famous in his department of art? And by what methods will he achieve his distinction? It is obvious that he will have to combine the powers of the dramatist, painter, and caricaturist with a peculiar capacity for making the world laugh at comedy expressed in the new terms of the motion picture.

Screen comedy as a composition must be distinguished from the art of acting in a screen comedy. Charlie Chaplin is a great screen comedian, but he has never yet acted in a great screen comedy. In fact the managers of Mr. Chaplin have taken the pains to show that a Chaplin comedy is a failure unless acted by Chaplin himself. On the other hand it has been shown repeatedly that, for example, a Molière comedy is successful even though acted by the veriest amateurs. Now if a screen comedy were distinctively comic in its essence, quite apart from its interpretation by actors, it would be produced at various times and by various companies, and might in the course of time be called a classic. Let us disabuse ourselves of the notion that any motion picture that makes us laugh is a screen comedy. A Dachshund or a mule colt pictured in action might make us laugh, and yet it would hardly be correct to say that a Dachshund or a mule colt was a screen comedy. Comic actors, comic animals, comic costumes, comic settings, comic incidents, comic situations, comic characters,— all these things are merely the materials out of which comedy may be built. The comedy itself is an arrangement of screen comics so composed that the presentation makes an audience laugh. And in so far as the laughter is due to the work and art of the composer, in so far may the play itself be called a good comedy. Let us say that laughter is caused by the perception of a spontaneously diverting incongruity. Then a comedy is a unified combination of spontaneously diverting incongruities.

The cinema composer who wishes to succeed as a maker of comedy must learn the conditions under which comedy makes a successful appeal to an audience. In the first place the play, if it is pure comedy, must not arouse the emotions of the audience. Furthermore, it must divert them from themselves, from their own emotions. It must make them forget that they are sad, angry, discouraged, in love, or ready to sacrifice themselves for their country. Second, it must not appeal to their reason; it must not start their brains puzzling over any problem. Third, it must make the laughter worth while; that is, it must not leave the audience sorry or ashamed that they have laughed.

Caprice, sportiveness, lack of seriousness is fundamentally necessary in a comedy, as in any comic effect. If you felt sorry for Charlie Chaplin you would not laugh at the thing that made you sorry for him. We laugh at the ludicrous distresses in comedy because we know that they are unattended by fatal consequences. We are diverted by the incongruities attached to characters, only when we have no serious emotional interest in those characters. In real life no devoted lover would be amused by something that made his sweetheart seem ridiculous, and no devout Christian would be amused by a jocular remark about God. So in literature we should not, for example, be amused by *The Legend of Sleepy Hollow* if we really worried over the fate of Ichabod Crane, or by Falstaff's lies, if we really resented his generous deviations from the strict truth. Here is the sharp distinction between comedy on the one hand and tragedy or serious drama on the other. "In serious drama, as we shall show in the chapter on " Dramatic Appeal," the writer should make every effort to get the audience emotionally interested in one or more of the characters of the play; but in comedy the writer must carefully forestall any possibility of the spectator's emotional concern. The spectator wants to be diverted from, not converted to, any emotional experience. The scenario writer, therefore, must weave his comedy out of the light, playful, whimsical tissues of harmless incongruities.

A very difficult thing in dramatic composition is the interweaving of the comic with the tragic. Shakespeare's method was to amuse the audience by the antics of clowns, servants, and underlings, while he kept them seriously interested in the characters and fates of kings, princes, generals, lords, and women of their social order.   This method may be used by the cinema composer, providing he does not let the comic episodes fall entirely out of key with the serious part of the drama.   Disjointed effects and absurd clashes will always be seen on the screen so long as one scenario writer attempts to write the serious part of the play, and another one the comic, or so long as studios purchase serious plays and attempt to improve them by putting in a dash of pseudo-comic relief here and there. Life itself makes a subtle mingling of the serious and comic, of tears and laughter; and a personality in which seriousness and humour are properly balanced can always make a strong appeal to our hearts.   But in life and in the theatre we are not both amused and made serious at the very same moment by the very same stimulus.   We are amused only when the comic has diverted us, snatched us away from our seriousness. The cinema composer will do well to study the technique of Dickens' novels, or of such a play as Charles Klein's *The Music Master*.   This play won its long popularity through the heart appeal of its hero, Herman von Barwig, the music master.   Thousands of audiences have wept at the pathetic situation of this old man.   Yet at every performance the pathos was merrily punctuated by laughter at the many funny things in the play.   Audiences laughed at the way spaghetti was eaten, at the way water went into the wine, at the way von Barwig's button hole must have " healed up," at the way he lost his coat through the attic window, at his droll remarks in the German idiom. None of these incongruities mattered much; they only diverted the audience from their emotional interest in the hero's feeling toward his long lost wife, and his new found daughter. But there was no joking on the topic of tears, at the old man's profound love, or at his refined taste in music; such jokes would have fallen flat. Such jokes, however, in some play of Mr. and Mrs. Sidney Drew, where no emotional interest is allowed to creep in, might bring forth hilarious laughter. The scenario writer must remember, therefore, when he undertakes to interweave the comic with the tragic, that, although the comic must divert us from the tragic, the two elements must be so organized that a single unity results.

Another condition of successful comedy is that there shall be no appeal to our reason. Comedy fails if it instantly stimulates thought instead of laughter. Sometimes we sit solemnly through an intended comic effect and exclaim, "How absurd!" Such an utterance results from a bit of reasoning, a judgment on our part. We have compared the supposedly comic incongruity with its corresponding norm, and the improbability was so extravagant that we refused to laugh. The absurdity which passes beyond laughter may be illustrated by a school boy's chalk drawing of a man with a nose ten times as long as his body. A cartoonist can call forth the desired smile by drawing the man's nose only twice its normal size. There may still be exaggeration but there is so much truth, too, that we accept, and are amused by, the incongruity and do not stop to reason about it. The comedy composer must not allow his audience to become resentful or argumentative at the moment when they should lose themselves to whole-hearted laughter.   He may deal with extravagances, to be sure, but they must be surrounded by an atmosphere that puts the audience into a receptive mood.   The stage play *Peter Pan* contains many extravagances, yet no audience ever stops to reason about them.   Barrie made his crocodile swallow an alarm clock; the writer of cheap photoplays would make his crocodile swallow an eight day clock from grandfather's hallway; one is amusing, the other is absurd.

Thirdly, comedy to be successful should evoke laughter worth while, the laughter one does not regret.   It may be said, of course, that all laughter, in so far as it is physically refreshing and tonic, is worth while.   Yet, the comedy that is endearing, the comedy we send our friends to see and will gladly see again ourselves, is the comedy that contains, not only the joy of life, but the truth of life as well.   We may even say that the best comedies contain the simple, working-day ideals of life.   We are amused by Molière's *The Imaginary Invalid* because so many of us have our little imaginary ailments, and as soon as we are through laughing at the comedy we make up our minds that we will never allow ourselves to become as ridiculous as the imaginary invalid.   We are amused at the blustering, braggart Bob Acres in Sheridan's *The Rivals* because we know from the beginning that he is an arrant coward, and because the incongruity contains a true picture of some of us; not you or me, of course, because, rather than be laughed at we are always determined to make good our every boast.   Thus at all the unfitness of things in comedy we laugh because we know better;

that " knowing better " is our ideal. George Meredith in a very interesting essay entitled *On the Uses of the Comic Spirit* says, " The use of true comedy is to awaken thoughtful laughter." We will accept that doctrine providing we may add that the thoughtfulness should come after the laughter and not during it. Thus comedy may satirize the amusing foibles, the silly shortcomings, the ludicrous uglinesses of humanity, providing the satire be so light that we do not start philosophizing when we should be laughing, and so poignant that, from our laughing at others, we may sober down into less ridiculous selves.

But let us pass from these general conditions to the more specific conditions of successful screen comedy. The comedy composer for the screen must be aware of his limitations. A great limitation is the absence of sound. "Much of the comic effect in a stage play is due to the tone, intonations, accent, and peculiar tricks of the comedian's voice." Another great limitation is the almost total absence of words. What fun is Micawber, or Mrs. Malaprop, or Bob Acres, or Falstaff without words? What can the screen substitute for the brilliant dialog of Sheridan and Wilde, for the caustic wit of Shaw? We can only repeat what we have said in the previous chapter that the composition of pictures in motion is an entirely different art from the composition of words, and that from the very nature of the two arts many of the comic effects of literature cannot be reproduced in screen comedy.

But as a compensation for these limitations the cinema composer has at his disposal many comic effects which are unique in screen comedy and cannot be produced in any other art. In the first place a comic effect for the screen needs to be performed only once, and that single performance caught by the camera can be repeated to audiences indefinitely by constant reprinting from the original negative. The director may have to experiment a great many times with his actors, animals, and objects before he arrives at that single satisfactory performance; but once the amusing result is obtained it need never be obtained again. ❝Compare this with the comic effects of the stage play which must be so conceived that they may be repeated every afternoon and evening during the entire run of the play.❞ The possibility of selecting and making permanent one comic performance, the most comic one out of many, is a tremendous advantage to such an actor as Charlie Chaplin.   He may undertake the most ridiculous posture or acrobatic "stunt."   If it fails or results disastrously the negative may be destroyed and he may try again; no audience need ever know of his failures.

Another unique possibility of the screen is the employment of animals for humorous effect.   Any subject may be presented, from a cockroach to a crocodile, from a turtle to an elephant, from a monkey to a mule. Nothing is so small that it cannot be shown in a close-up; nothing is so slow that the director cannot wait for its part in the comedy.   Who has not seen the mirthful laughter of children at the frisky pranks or droll behaviour of dogs and kittens, of pigs and calves and colts?   None of these comic values may be reproduced on the stage; all of them may be reproduced on the screen.

The employment of animals for comic effect would not be possible without the cinema selection spoken of in the preceding paragraph. But it is not enough merely to wait until the animal does something funny. This humorous effect must be woven into the comedy, or comic portion of the serious play, as an essential part of the entire pattern. We have already discussed the dramatization of animals in the chapter on " Dramatizing a Natural Setting," and shall only add another example here. The Fox photoplay *The Honor System* has a very vivid presentation of conditions in the penitentiary of one of our Southwestern states. One can almost smell the dirt, or hear the gnawing rats and buzzing flies that surround the poor prisoners. Not least in evidence are the large cockroaches crawling along the prison bars. Some prisoner of a practical mind and a sense of humour has put the cockroaches into service as the mail carriers of the penitentiary, a device which gives comic relief during periods of depression. The prisoner writes his message on a tiny piece of paper which he wets and sticks to the mail carrier's back; the faithful cockroach wanders around among the cells and finally delivers his message. One day a mutiny is brewing among the convicts and the hour for striking is imminent. The leader of the gang writes the significant words " Tomorrow at six " on a piece of paper and sticks it to the faithful mail carrier, who puts on full speed and, to the consternation of the convict, makes straight for the guard, who is dozing in the sun. Up the guard's back he goes and straight for his ear. Things look black for the mutineers. But at the critical moment the cockroach, as though he, too, had a sense of humour, executes " about face " and delivers the message first to one convict then to another until his long task is complete.

Here is a comic effect original and of the cinema cinematic. It diverts the audience in a new way, and relieves the strain during a tense dramatic situation.

The composer of screen comedy may even draw his material from the realm of the inanimate. In a Chaplin comedy, for example, the hero's hat, or coat, or cane, a tiger skin rug, a swinging door, or a folding bed, all may play the rôles of comedians. In a stage play one could not always be sure that these mere things would perform the comic feats assigned to them; but if they can be made to do the trick once in the motion picture studio that is enough for the screen comedy. And by means of camera magic, as we have shown in a previous chapter, almost any action, ridiculous or otherwise, can be performed by inanimate objects.

Even the setting itself may assume the character of jester. For example, in one of Max Linder's screen comedies, entitled *Max Comes Across,* the pitching and rolling of an ocean liner is realistically represented as it is experienced by those on board. At one time we see a fat woman jolted out of the upper berth in her cabin, at another time the passengers are seen at dinner struggling with clownishly active dishes and agile viands, keeping their seats with difficulty as the deck wabbles beneath them, and later when Max undertakes to play at the ship's concert, we behold the grand piano dart back and forth, dancing idiotically to the motions of the sea.

Comic effects may further be produced by giving humorous exaggeration to the powers of man or beast. Thus some drunken ruffian standing in the middle of the road may swear that he can halt the speeding auto-

mobile by simply seizing it with his good right hand.
He not only makes good his boast by stopping the car
but he hurls it backward so hard that it doesn't stop for
six blocks.   Or Reynard the cunning fox pounces upon
Chanticler the vain cock and with one powerful shake
of his jaws completely strips poor Chanticler of his
feathers and scatters them to the four winds of heaven.
Or our Fido starts barking savagely at a decrepit railroad train standing unsuspecting at the station and
frightens it so that it scampers down the track at full
speed to some safer place.

¶The possibility of accelerating or retarding normal
speed is a whole region of comedy in itself." In fact
much unintended comedy results from the failure to
represent rate of movement truthfully on the screen.
A familiar fiasco is the picture of troops marching off
to the front.   The dignity, solemnity, and sadness is
too often turned into farce by a rapid film which makes
the men hop along like jumping-jacks.   On the other
hand retardation of normal speed may also have amusing results.   Who has not heard titters at some soul-
stirring grand opera when a beautiful property bird
flies heavily and much too slowly over the singers.
Similar unmeant comedy may often be seen in cheap
photoplays.   But the observant composer may profit
by such fiascos.   The thing which fails in a serious
play may be a huge success in a comedy.   In fact several film corporations are now reissuing as burlesques
the very same pictures which a few years ago were
solemnly presented as serious plays.   By cutting in a
few farcical sub-titles here and there and speeding up
the projection a bit one can easily turn these early
melodramas into burlesques.   In plays originally con-

ceived as comedies the deviation from normal speed may often produce laughable incongruity. An elephant may trip along as lightly as a spaniel, and a spaniel may lumber along as bulkily as an elephant.

The greatest function of comedy is, of course, the delineation of comic characters in comic situations. And in this respect screen comedy, though it must dispense with voice and speech, can do many things impossible in the stage play. None of the visual values of acting need ever be lost. The actor's posture and movement may be photographed from any ridiculous angle and his slyest wink and tiniest grimace may be caught in a close-up. Furthermore a comic character has an almost unlimited scope of action in a photoplay. An absent-minded man can be absent-minded more often and about more different things than in a stage play. A vulgar woman with polite pretensions can make her *faux pas* in more places and under more varying circumstances; the painfully prim old maid can be shocked by more situations; the pompous braggart can be exposed to more tests, and the gawking country cousin can be confronted with more amazing things in the photoplay than in the stage play. With few exceptions the clowns, buffoons, Merry-Andrews, and mirth-provoking idiots known in life or literature can be marshalled before us on the screen in side-splitting array and put through their paces in an uproarious procession. And it is not too much to expect that the cinema composer, with so many unique powers in his command, will present novel aspects of the ridiculous in life, will present people who are fools in a new way, or create characters who are witty in a new language.

When the ordinary resources of the motion picture play are exhausted the man with ideas for comic plots may turn to the animated cartoons. In the animated cartoons any impossibility may become possible. The genius of the grotesque may produce things that act like animals, rabbits that act like Podunkville preachers, and men who literally wiggle their ears, or noses if need be. At present most of the artists who make animated cartoons invent their own plots, such as they are. But there is no reason why clever plot makers should not collaborate with cartoonists. There is also no reason why the animated cartoons should not occasionally rise above vulgar horse-play. Perhaps some day some one will conjure up on the screen such whimsical and delightful fancies as Sir James Barrie has conjured up on the stage.

We have surveyed briefly the main points in the field of screen comedy. It would be interesting to continue with a discussion of the technique of comedy in general, whether of the screen or of the stage, of such topics as the force of surprise, the effect of repetition and cumulation, the relation between comedy of incident, of situation, and of character, and the difference between farce and pure comedy, but space does not permit. Besides we have been told on good authority that a man who insists on analysing a joke is clearly without a sense of humour.

CHAPTER XI

THE DELINEATION OF CHARACTER

THUS we have studied the nature of the photoplay from many angles and have seen that the cinema composer has many opportunities and responsibilities as an artist in a new medium. But the sum of all his responsibilities, for which all his means are an end, is the impressive revelation of human character in action. And before he can reveal, he must create, dramatic character; for the rôle of the artist is never properly filled by mere slavish copying of people in real life. A dramatic character is a person with a personality which dominates a plot, or is itself dominated by a plot, or is in mutual reaction with the plot. The two essentials are personality and action.

Personality, individuality is that something which differentiates Napoleon from Wellington, Goethe from Schiller, Hamlet from Othello, Juliet from Ophelia and any one of us from the others. That something results from a peculiar combination of physical aspects or attributes with intellectual or spiritual qualities. This particular make-up of characteristics differing from all other make-ups, constitutes individuality. Unfortunately most photoplays contain mere persons instead of characters, persons who have not yet matured into personalities. A broad-shouldered man without any other distinguishing quality reveals no more personality than a clothier's advertisement of a

mannikin in a $23.00 suit.   A pretty girl in a poster
may have prettiness, a smile and a regular curve from
temple to chin, but, like a doll, usually lacks personality.
An art critic looking at such a picture would immediately say that it "lacks character."   A single physical
aspect is not enough to give individuality.   Strength,
skill, weakness, grace, slenderness, bowleggedness, a
hunched back, a big jaw, a fifty-inch belt, arched eyebrows, a quivering mouth, a flashing eye, a wabbly
step, a cigarette flicking hand — none of these alone
constitutes a combination, and therefore none of these
alone is sufficient to distinguish a character.

The proper method of producing unique combinations of aspects, attributes, and traits may be learned
by studying successful writers of fiction.   Here, as an
illustration, is a paragraph from Bret Harte's *The Luck
of Roaring Camp:*   " The assemblage numbered about
a hundred men.   One or two of these were actual fug-
itives from justice, some were criminal, and all were
reckless.   Physically, they exhibited no indication of
their past lives and character.   The greatest scamp
had a Raphael face, with a profusion of blonde hair;
Oakhurst, a gambler, had the melancholy air and intellectual abstraction of a Hamlet; the coolest and most
courageous man was scarcely over five feet in height,
with a soft voice and an embarrassed, timid manner.
The term ' roughs ' applied to them was a distinction
rather than a definition.   Perhaps in the minor details
of fingers, toes, ears, etc., the camp may have been
deficient, but these slight omissions did not detract
from the aggregate force.   The strongest man had but
three fingers on his right hand; the best shot had but
one eye."   This concise description of novel combina-

tions of appearance and attributes make it easy for the reader to visualize Harte's inhabitants of Roaring Camp as individuals and not as general types. Of course, the author's delineation of character does not stop with the paragraph quoted; if it did the characterization would not be complete. A three-fingered expert marksman is not by virtue of that distinction alone a definite character. Photoplaywrights and directors too often assume that the physical distinction of the actor or actress may be substituted for individuality of character in the plot. The physical appearance may indeed symbolize the inner man; but this inner man is a bundle of invisible though perceptible things. His temperament is phlegmatic or enthusiastic, melancholy or irritable. He possesses some definite trait of disposition: kindness or rudeness, geniality or snobbishness. He has some definite habit of mind: suspicion, jealousy, impulsiveness, gullibility, imaginativeness, vacillation, or deliberateness. In moral fibre he may be upright or unscrupulous, selfish, untruthful, or envious. Thus we might go on until we had exhausted all the appropriate nouns, adjectives, and adverbs in the unabridged dictionary. A character needs not, of course, many different characteristics. He need not be complex, but he must represent an individual combination, otherwise he is not a character at all.

The searching out and assembling of materials for the creation of character is a profound joy to the genuine author. His sources are everywhere about him. In some drama he discovers a minor character whose story possibility has not been exploited; in some art gallery he glimpses a subtle trait in an old portrait; in his newspaper he reads of an interesting though obscure character or of some prominent man revealed by his acts; in some book of history he ponders over the tragic motives of famous or notorious women; in the vast, never-ending panorama of real life he studies his casual acquaintances, his friends, himself; and from all these sources he selects and combines just two or three traits, two or three physical aspects, into a new character, who in time gets into a series of happenings and thus becomes the core of a play.

While the cinema composer is at work on this new character he must see to it that he makes the personality both interesting and convincing.   That the personality be fascinating, absorbing, is especially important commercially, because it is only such a part that appeals to the ambitious actor or actress.   And what the great performer loves to interpret the discriminating audience loves to behold.   Whether the character be good or bad makes no difference so long as it is distinctive and interesting; the unscrupulous Lady Macbeth is no less fascinating than the charming Viola, and the hardened Mrs. Warren is no less absorbing than the conventional Mrs. Alving.

But originality of conception must never be allowed to pass the bounds of convincingness.   The combination of qualities should be one which might probably exist in life.   A convincing, life-like portrait looks as though it might step out of the frame; so a convincing character should look as though he might step out of the scenario on to the screen; for a cinematic character should have a definite entity quite apart from the reality given by the actor, should have body and soul, sins and virtues, distinct individuality, a past, present and future long before the actor knows of his existence. And when this character is shadowed forth on the screen he should be recognized at once by the audience as a faithful delineation of an interesting and highly probable real human being.

The relation between character and action will be discussed at some length in the chapter on " Dramatic Appeal," where it will be shown that the audience may be kept in suspense wondering what the character will turn out to be, whether he will remain what he is, or will change under the influence of the action in which he is involved. And the further relation between character and plot will be alluded to in the chapter on " The Construction of a Plot." In fact it is not really possible to speak of character and plot as though they existed separately in the play. Incident, action is of no interest except with relation to character, and dramatic character cannot be finally revealed except through action.

The main problem in the photoplay is to give the audience sufficient knowledge of the character to become personally interested in him. Without this intimacy there can be no social emotion, no dramatic sympathy. But the means for bringing about this acquaintance is limited in the motion pictures. There is no such latitude as in the stage play where the audience may know the character through his dialog, comments, promises, threats, declarations; through his expressed attitude toward other characters and their expressed attitude toward him; through his antecedent acts as described in the dialog of himself or others; through the physical environment which he has created or to which he reacts; and first, last, and always through his physical appearance, physical expression, and action.

Nor is there the scope of the novel where the ever-increasing riches of language are drawn upon to express the most curious eccentricities, the profoundest depths, the noblest heights, and the most delicate shadings of human character.

The cinema composer in delineating character must almost entirely dispense with words; yet, if he draws upon the peculiar and manifold powers of his medium, he may make photoplay characters as vivid and impressive in their way as any other characters in art. In the first place the author of a photoplay, like the author of a stage play, should conceive the type of character who reveals himself by the things he does, by his action, and who will be further revealed by the actor's interpretation of the part. "Visible action and visible acting may be more fully descriptive on the screen than on the stage, because the photoplay can present more action in more places than the stage play, and the cinematograph can record the droop of an eyelash so slight that it would be unseen on the stage." In this respect the photoplay director can surely better the instruction of his immediate ancestor, the stage director.

In addition the cinema composer may play the rôle of portrait painter. Let him obey the principles of pictorial composition in static forms, repeating a phase of expression until it impresses the spectators, organizing all the powers of tone and texture and line, relating the central character to his dramatic group, dramatizing his setting until it is more expressive than any setting ever copied on canvas, always investing beauty for the eye with meaning for the mind of the spectator.

The cinema author-director-painter may be sculptor too. While a painting can be viewed only from a single fixed point of vision, a piece of sculpture can and must be viewed from many distances and many angles. An observer can walk completely around a statue and thus see hundreds of slightly different aspects of the same subject. Apply this test to Rodin's *Le Penseur*, for example, and you will discover that this silent man, The Thinker, is thoughtful with every part of his body; the eyebrows, the fists, the toes, the back — all reveal him as deeply thoughtful. Painters sometimes imitate the method of the sculptor by placing their subject beside a mirror, thus revealing to the beholder an additional aspect in the reflected image. And this trick of the painter has in turn been imitated thousands of times on the screen. But the photoplay may go even farther than this; it may in a sense show sculpture in motion. It may present the subject at many distances and from many angles, physically and dramatically as well, emphasizing again and again the fundamental differentiating traits of the character until the audience is unforgetably impressed with the dramatic personality. Furthermore, the author-director-painter-sculptor may turn symbolist, devising new symbols for cinematic expression, or investing old symbols with new meaning in the delineation of character. And, finally, in addition to all his expression in visible forms, he may in a unique way deftly lead the spectator to imagine the unexpressed traits and nature of the dramatic character.

All these means of cinematic expression have been elucidated in preceding chapters, and mere allusion to them is sufficient now. But it may prove interesting to study some particular means of delineating character on the screen. For the sake of convenience we may divide the determining characteristics of a person into visibilities and invisibilities. Absent-mindedness, for example, is a visibility, visible through the physical appearance of the actor, and visible in the acts which the character performs. But, for example, undue optimism is not a visibility; it cannot be seen directly with the eye, but is to be inferred rather from the spoken or written words of the optimist. Hence Micawber is not a suitable character for the screen. In the same way we may divide states of the mind into visibilities and invisibilities, and we may say, for example, that being angry is visible, and remembering the past is not. "Now the stage play expresses visibilities through action, and invisibilities through dialog; but since dialog is taboo on the screen a satisfactory cinematic substitute must be found."

Suppose that at some point in a photoplay our soldier-hero in the trenches remembers his sweetheart across the seas. The audience must be able to see that he remembers and see what he remembers. And the cinema composer solves the problem by the simple, already conventional, device of fading in a vision of the girl against some flat surface, say the wall of a dugout, at which the hero is looking. The skilful composer may devise some less hackneyed way of representing memory, as we may illustrate by a scene from a photoplay entitled *The Lost Bridegroom*. In this play the hero on his way home from his bachelor dinner is waylaid by thugs, partly stripped, and so badly beaten up that he forgets his identity. He wanders into a saloon, where he is mistaken for a prize-fighter, and is engaged as official " bouncer." In the course of a few days he has acquired the rowdyest kind of dress and physical appearance. He has lost his identity, and the bride will have to wait in vain until he finds it. Now the author wants to show the audience that on a certain morning the hero gradually remembers who he is. This is the way it is done. The hero, fully dressed in rough shirt and trousers, is standing before a mirror looking at his image. Gradually and dimly the image of the " bouncer " changes to that of a man in a dress suit, the hero as he appeared on the night when he was assaulted. The lost bridegroom has now recovered his memory, and the author has only to depict the series of incidents in which he escapes from his menial position and recovers his bride.

Other invisible activities of a character's mind, such as hope, ambition, desire, planning for revenge, may be depicted by the same screen device of fading in and fading out. A servant girl standing in front of a modiste's window desires to wear that beautiful dress; fade in the girl's own image instead of the mannikin of the window. A man wants to kill his rival in a duel; show him fencing wildly against the empty air in his back yard, and fade in the poor enemy where the lunges are the fiercest. A society cracksman fears that the law will get him; fade in the hand-cuffs on his wrists. A lord desires to become king; fade in the crown upon his head.

All these are simple, and perhaps rather obvious, devices for expressing visually what is in the mind of the dramatic character. They are merely the beginnings, the A B C book words in a new language, the language of the motion picture play, an infant among the arts.

And even if the cinema composer, either through inventiveness or assimilation, commanded a large vocabulary in this new language of visual values it would be unwise for him to use it, for the audiences are still as mere beginners learning to read a new language. Beginners must familiarize themselves with the ordinary words and the short sentences before they can understand the more difficult, though more completely expressive, passages.   Now, the psychology of a person learning a new language is peculiar.   Let us say that an Englishman is learning French.   He will mentally formulate his thoughts in English first and then convert them into the corresponding French terms, or when hearing French, will convert the words separately into English.   A similar roundabout mental process is gone through by the average spectator at a photoplay.   He is accustomed to the terms of the stage play, of painting, of sculpture, of all the elder arts, and into these terms he first translates the cinematic expression whether it be crude or subtle, before he grasps the meaning intended by the cinema composer.   Hence it may take a generation, perhaps even half a century of training on the part both of authors and appreciators before the photoplay can develop unique descriptive power of a flavour and richness comparable with that of the elder arts.

Returning to the problem of delineating the invisibilities of human character we may observe that there really is no great difficulty, providing what the character is thinking about is concretely imaged.   But what can the camera do with vague emotions, fleeting notions, and inarticulate ideas?   For such things the dramatist or poet in their wizardry would somehow invent words, but words are not proper to the screen. The language of the screen should be in proper terms of the screen; and these terms may be found if we look long enough.   There is a photoplay entitled *The Painted Soul,* which depicts clearly to the audience a psychological change in the heroine so subtle that she herself is hardly aware of it.   An artist goes to a night court to select from the prisoners a suitable model for a picture which is to be called "The Fallen Woman." A prostitute is chosen.   She comes to his studio and is posed at a table, supposed to be in a disreputable restaurant, with a whiskey glass beside her, and a cigarette in her hand.   In the midst of the first sitting the artist is called out of the studio.   The girl rummages around and finds his watch and chain, which she hides in her dress.   Her curiosity further leads her to pull aside the draperies from a large painting.   She gazes at it and is gradually spellbound by the artist's conception of a pure woman, the Madonna.   This painting is so placed that it is directly across the room from the model-stand, and the girl rests her eyes on it when she resumes her sitting.   The first effect is that she surreptitiously restores the watch.   But a more subtle effect comes during subsequent sittings when it is evident to the audience that the prostitute is gradually approximating the pose and assuming the expression of the painted Madonna.   This, of course, totally unfits the model for the painting of "The Fallen Woman," and the artist gives it up, blaming himself for lack of skill, and never perceives the true cause of his failure.   Here is a simple but truly cinematic delineation of a spiritual invisibility which distinguishes a character in a genuine dramatic situation.

Let us close our ears then to the Philistine who says that the photoplay may well present stirring pictures of cowboy races or Mexican battles but cannot undertake to delineate the inner nature of men or convey the drama of souls.   For we have already caught a glimpse here and there of what the future cinema-dramatist may do if he brings inventiveness to sincerity and inspiration to both.

CHAPTER XII

DRAMATIC APPEAL

AFTER the photoplaywright gets a general knowledge and command of his medium, understands the principles of composition in static and fluent forms, can practise camera magic, can wield photographic realities so that they suggest the imaginary, can invent or energize symbols, can dramatize setting, can fuse words with pictures, can produce comedy, can delineate character on the screen, he faces the problem of utilizing all or most of these means in order to make a dramatic appeal to his audience. To make this dramatic appeal he will have to construct his play as deliberately as if he were the architect of a house. An architect has to recognize and obey certain unchanging laws of gravitation, equilibrium, tension, and stress. He has no choice in the matter. He cannot alter, ignore, or repeal these laws. In the same way the author must recognize and obey the laws of the human mind, laws which have not changed since the world began. People become interested, pay attention, get excited and calm down, remember and forget in exactly the same way today as when the first savage told a story or scratched the rude picture of a beast on the wall of a cave. Hence it is that the artist yet unborn may go to school to the artist long since dead. Hence it is, also, that two different arts utilize the same principle of mental appeal and still remain distinct as arts. We have already contended that the cinema play is a new art distinct from all the other arts which were invented and have been developed before it. We have further maintained the proposition that the cinema composer can learn his lessons and adopt his methods from the masters in other arts. Let him finish his training by studying the principles of spoken drama and the laws of dramatic appeal.

" Dramatic appeal is based on plot; without plot there could be no dramatic appeal. " Without plot the photoplay is merely a succession of pictures, the stage play is merely a parade of unrelated actions. What is " plot," and when may the term be applied to a series of happenings? A plot can not be constructed by merely arranging happenings in a progressive order. The events recounted in a biography are usually in a progressive order; yet no biography, however interesting, can be said to have plot. Progression in time alone has, of course, no plot value. Nobody is interested in observing that Tuesday follows Monday, and that Wednesday follows Tuesday, or that youth follows babyhood, and maturity, youth. Nor is the fulfilment of expectation in itself a plot. We are not held by plot interest when we watch the budding and blossoming of a rose or the ripening of an apple. If we did not know whether the bud would become an apple or an acorn, or whether the boy would become a priest or a policeman, we should be more interested in the development. We should then experience something like plot interest. "Plot interest is a blending of the expected with the unexpected." From a given cause we are led to expect certain effects, but the effects come in an unexpected way which pleases us. Or we observe a given unexpected effect and remark that with a little more shrewdness we might have expected that effect from the given cause. In a plot the progression of happenings must be in a logical sequence of cause and effect. Yet the logic must not be so mathematical that the conclusion is foregone, that there is no chance for the unexpected. The happenings must put us in a state of suspense, in a questioning frame of mind; yet it must be almost possible to relieve that suspense by reasoning concerning the facts before us. For example, in *Romeo and Juliet* we learn first that two Italian families are in a feud, then that the son of one family is in love with the daughter of the other family. As soon as we are in possession of these initial facts we can foresee a number of possible complications, but we cannot be sure which ones will follow; we cannot prophesy with certainty. Presently we see what the lovers are planning to do, and our suspense increases. Their secret marriage relieves part of our suspense by answering some of our questions, but it also gives rise to new questions and new suspense. Thus our interest leaps forward to the possible outcome, and our attention remains intent on the action lest some detail may escape us. During all this progress of happenings one general question is present in our minds. It might be phrased as follows: "How can Romeo and Juliet be permanently and peacefully united while their parents are enemies?" This is the main dramatic problem. The only solution is death. The last scene of the play relieves all suspense, and, curiously enough, satisfies our emotions.

Perhaps this brief discussion of what constitutes

plot interest will enable us to arrive at a working definition of plot as used in a photoplay. A cinema plot is a progression of pictured happenings or conditions in a logical sequence contrived to create and relieve suspense in the mind of the spectator. Let us emphasize the terms " progression," " logical sequence," and " suspense." If a given series of "pictured happenings " possess these qualities they may be said to have plot. And plot is the basic factor in dramatic appeal.

We say that the cinema play is "dramatic " in its method of appeal because, like the stage play, it presents physically before our eyes the happenings of a human action in plot form. It *shows* the story which the novel can only *tell*. It mimics through the agency of living human beings the plot which the author has woven around the beings of his imagination. Therefore the spectator becomes the witness of a section of life enacted either on the screen or on the stage; and what he sees puts him into a state of suspense.

The cinema play, like the stage play, sets life before us in pantomime. But since people in real life talk while they act, the author of a plot must let us either hear or read or imagine the words which accompany the deeds of his characters. In spoken drama the playwright needs only to make pantomime reinforce his dialog. His pantomime need not be self-explanatory. But cinematic pantomime must translate into terms of physical expression the meanings which the playwright puts into words. The pantomime must be in itself sufficient to convey the plot to the spectator, as well as to reveal to him the individual personalities of the chief figures in that plot. If occasionally a phrase or sentence must be projected on the screen in order to clarify the story, such a cinematic device must be looked upon as merely an exceptional auxiliary, used only when the power of pantomime is exhausted.

But the scenario writer must not make the mistake of confusing acting with physical action. "Acting is merely the performer's interpretation of any given action." Whether this interpretation is crude or artistic, finished or amateurish, the action remains basically the same action. It is independent of the actor and exists before he begins to interpret the play. The writer has conceived these actions and given them dramatic significance. If the play contains a kiss or a prize fight, the plucking of a daisy or the charge of an infantry brigade, it is because the writer has decided that this action is essential to the plot. Even in the stage play where pantomime is not so important as in the photoplay it is often deliberately put in by the playwright. Look through the stage directions of any play by Bernard Shaw, for instance *Cæsar and Cleopatra,* and you will observe how carefully the author has specified actions and bits of "stage business" which advance plot and reveal character. "Study the usage of Shakespeare in presenting such characters as Richard III, Falstaff, or the shrewish Katherine and you will see that he considered pantomime almost as important as words." In Galsworthy's *Justice* the most dramatic scene of the whole play, the prison scene showing Falder alone in his cell, is all pantomime, no word being spoken. It is obvious that in all these cases the physical dramatic action is inherent in the play, and is not contributed by the actor, though it may be interpreted by him." All the respon-

sibility, therefore, of composing a series of pantomimed actions into a dramatic plot should rest upon
the scenario writer.   His three-fold problem, stated
concisely, is, to conceive pantomimed actions that are
self-explanatory and progressive in meaning; that adequately portray the personalities of the characters; and
that keep the spectators in a state of suspense as to the
outcome of the plot.

" To produce suspense must be the primary aim of the
plot maker." If he cannot keep the audience in suspense during the unfolding of his action he cannot
hold their attention at all.   This tension of the mind
is not so necessary in other forms of art.   A painting
requires no suspense because it is not necessary that
the beholder look upon it for any given length of time.
It is entirely optional with him whether he shall spend
an hour or a minute in receiving the message of the
artist.   The same option obtains in the case of the
novel.   The reader may take it portion by portion,
three pages or three chapters, and at any time.   But
no such option is possible when a story is represented
on the stage or on the screen.   Every individual in
the theatre must, so to speak surrender his watch to
the author, who times the period of the spectator's attention.   The problem of making all the individuals of
the audience fix their attention on the same subject for
the same length of time can be solved by the secret of
dramatic suspense.

"Suspense may be defined as a mental state of alert
expectancy and doubt. " We are alert to every turn and
twist and forward movement of the plot because we
expect interesting developments, but we are kept in a
state of uncertainty and doubt as to what they will be

and when they will come. There is always a race between our attention and the movement of a story, whether the story is unfolding on the screen, on the stage, or in a book. Suppose that we are reading a novel at the rate of a page a minute. The plot, then, is moving forward at the rate of a page a minute. But if our mind is confused, perplexed, or bored, our attention lags behind the plot. We are still back perhaps on page 90 while the plot is passing beneath our eyes on page 100. In some other novel the plot is too obvious, and our mind, anticipating the outcome, wins the race. It easily guesses the action of the last chapter while our eyes are still on the chapter next to the last. But when our mind tries in vain to outstrip the plot, tries in vain to get to the end of the story before the action itself gets there, the result is a state of perfect suspense.

Suspense always takes the form of a question with an answer always more or less remotely out of reach. Let us examine the *Merchant of Venice* to see what questions the playwright plants in the mind of the audience. The list is somewhat as follows: 1. Why is Antonio sad? 2. How will Bassanio get funds? 3. Will the love lottery be fortunate for Portia? 4. Will Shylock get revenge? 5. What will happen if Shylock's daughter marries a Christian? 6. No. 3 again. 7. No. 4 again. 8. No. 3 again. 9. No. 4 again. 10. Will Bassanio choose the right casket? 11. Will Shylock accept Portia's money? 12. What adventures will Portia and Nerissa have in disguise? 13. Will Shylock insist on his revenge? 14. How will the presence of the disguised Portia affect the trial? 15. If Antonio dies how will his fate affect

Bassanio and Portia? 16. How will Bassanio discover the identity of the clever lawyer? 17. What fibs will Bassanio and Gratiano tell their wives about the rings? As soon as these questions are answered suspense is relieved and our plot interest has run its course. It will be observed that some of the above questions are more persistent than others, and that some answers are deferred longer than others. The issue of the pound of flesh looms above all others in importance. It grips our attention and holds it firmly. Our hopes and fears are evenly balanced and we are alert with eyes and ears for any scrap of evidence that will swing the arm of the scales. We are most alert during the trial scene at the moment when Antonio bares his breast for the knife of Shylock. And our tension is relaxed when the quick wit of Portia saves the merchant's life. All the ensuing action comes merely as a pleasant epilogue to a tense, well-sustained dramatic situation.

If you review the questions set down above you will realize that they are organized questions, that the plot of the *Merchant of Venice* is a well-woven fabric in which every thread of interest is an organic part of the main pattern. "The result is a dramatic unity, a singleness of purpose without which the attention of the spectator could not have been firmly held." The scenario writer should strive for a similar unity in his succession of pictures. No matter how far apart the settings may be and how dissimilar the actions may seem, the various pictures should heighten suspense with reference to some main question in the plot.

The play we have just analysed illustrates the simplest type of suspense, the forward interest, the re-

peated question " What will happen next? "   There is
another type of suspense, a backward interest, the
retrospective question " What has already happened? "
To a slight degree this interest is present when we
see the *Merchant of Venice*.   What has happened to
make Antonio sad?   How has he offended Shylock?
When did the romance of Portia and Bassanio begin?
This double interest can be made a very subtle thing
in drama.   It is as though the audience, travelling the
road to tomorrow, turned occasionally for a glance
down the road to yesterday.   Some plays are so constructed that the road to tomorrow leads uphill.   As
we ascend this road, we may look back upon the road
to yesterday which opens and lengthens as it stretches
back through the plain of the past.   Thus we traverse
with our eyes a road which our feet do not tread.
" This type of retrospective suspense can easily be
aroused and maintained in the drama of words, but not
in the drama of pictures." It is only by the most skilful use of devices that the cinema composer can make
his story go backwards as well as forwards.   As long
as the pictures shown on the screen represent actions
in their chronological order, the spectator may easily
follow the story.   But when the succession of pictures
do not present the actions in the order in which they
are supposed to have happened in life the spectator
immediately becomes confused.

The secret of the difficulty is that an action represented in a picture has only the present tense, while
an action represented in a verb has a past and a future
tense as well as the present.   An action in a picture
on the screen is always taking place while we are looking at it.   It has neither past tense nor future tense.

If we see a picture of a wedding we infer that the man and woman are being married now, not that they were married ten years ago, or that they will be married next June. "But in the drama of words the verbs unmistakably tell us whether the action is in the present, in the past, or in the future."

We do not encourage the cinema composer to undertake the development of retrospective suspense in the photoplay; but for the sake of completeness in this chapter we shall illustrate how that dramatic effect is produced in the spoken drama.   In Ibsen's *Ghosts* the most dramatic part of the action has taken place before the curtain rises, and the play is really the climax of these actions which we hear about, and therefore imagine, but never see before us on the stage.   While we behold a succession of actions on the stage, the dialog of the characters carry our minds back sometimes ten years, sometimes twenty-seven, sometimes twenty.   And the play gains in dramatic impressiveness because certain facts are held back from the audience until the psychological moment for discovery. The following is a list of the antecedent happenings set down in the order in which the audience learns of them.   Note that the numbers in parentheses indicate the chronological positions of the happenings as they actually took place.   (3) Within a year after the marriage Mrs. Alving left her husband, but was urged by Pastor Manders to go back.   (1) Captain Alving was a libertine even as a bridegroom.   (7) Oswald Alving was sent off in early childhood to be reared away from home.   (8) After a married life of about eighteen years Captain Alving died unregenerate; but his wife had white washed his name after his death as well as during the latter years of his life. (5) Captain Alving has had a union with Mrs. Alving's maid. The illegitimate child of this union was Regina, Mrs. Alving's present maid. (6) Jacob Engstrand had been bribed to marry Regina's mother and pose as the father of the child. (2) Mrs. Engstrand had offered herself to Pastor Manders at the time when she left her husband. (9) Oswald had dissipated in Paris. (4) Oswald had inherited a disease from his father.

The audience is held in breathless suspense during this gradual discovery of the past. And this suspense is developed by the playwright's selective revelation and careful withholding of certain facts until the moment of greatest effectiveness. Interest gains in intensity because the audience is trying to look two ways at once. They are wondering what the dramatic characters will do in the future when they discover what has happened in the past. Yet, despite this complexity of attention, the audience is not confused. It classifies events in their proper places, no matter in what order they are presented; and the accuracy of the classification is assured by the accuracy of the language in the play.

But imagine the confusion of the audience if the events above described in words were to be photographed and presented in the order in which Ibsen presents them. The easiest way to avoid confusion in the cinema play when actions are interpolated out of their chronological order is to put a sub-title before the picture, stating just how long ago the action is supposed to have taken place. But such a device is itself a tribute to a certain superiority of words over pictures. The narration of the cinema play should be picture narration and not word narration. And the ethics of picture narration demands that the pictures be self-explanatory and establish their own coherence. For the present we are primarily concerned with the principle of dramatic suspense. If dramatic suspense can be heightened in the photoplay by a disarrangement of chronological order, well and good; if suspense cannot be heightened by such means, the chronological order should be adhered to because it guarantees clearness and smoothness in the story.

Before dismissing this subject of retrospective interest in recalled action of the spoken drama, we must point out one of the values of such action which the photoplay cannot easily parallel. "In such a play as *Ghosts* there are two kinds of action, the action which the characters perform on the stage, which we in the audience all see alike, and the action which these characters talk about as having happened in the past, which we in the audience, imagine, each one of us thinking of the action in terms of his own individual imagination." Thus our imaginations become constructive, helping the playwright in the building of his play. But when the mediocre photoplaywright wishes to present a past action, he usually projects it on the screen just as completely and accurately and realistically as the present action, thus eliminating from the play one of its elements of value, the opportunity for exercising the spectator's imagination.

The unimaginative, photographic restaging of the past was tried in the stage play *On Trial,* a play which has often been spoken of as having photoplay technique. In this play a man is being tried for murder.

His wife and daughter are called in as witnesses, and their testimony instead of being recited in words is re-enacted, everything being restored as in the past. The structure of Reizenstein's play may be represented graphically as follows: let D, E, and F represent the progress of the trial in the three acts of the play; and let a, b, and c represent the actions which took place before the trial begins. The play is constructed thus: $D(c)D$; $E(b)E$; $F(a)F$. c is like a cut-back re-enacting the events on the evening of the fatal day, including the shooting. b is the action of the afternoon a few hours before the shooting. And a is the action which took place thirteen years before the shooting. The second F is the end of the trial and the acquittal of the defendant. Thus the playwright started us at D and asked us to walk in two directions at once, forward to F and back to a. The experience was a novelty to the audience, and was not confusing because the interpolated action of the past was in each case clearly introduced by words. For example, in the first act the attorney says to the wife, " Will you tell the jury what you were doing on the evening of June 24th about 9:30 p. m.? " The woman starts to speak and immediately the trial scene becomes dark, the huge, revolving stage swings around to the setting of the woman's home, and the lights go up on the action of June 24th, where the witness herself, having made a quick change of costume, now participates. *On Trial* was a novelty to the audience, and as such was a commercial success, but the novelty did not become an innovation in the technique of the spoken drama. "Audiences, on the whole, seem to prefer the physical action which moves forward continuously." They may delight in imagining

or recalling vaguely the dead past, but they do not want
to relive it actually while they are living the present.
They may glance back wistfully over the road to yesterday, but they want to feel the road to tomorrow under their feet. "The photoplay is especially adapted to
present the plot which urges ever forward."

There are numerous ways of putting a spectator into
the state of suspense. It is not necessary always to
make him wonder *what* will happen or *what* has happened. "He may know what is going to happen and
yet be alertly waiting for the exact moment *when* it
will happen." The suspense is most intense when the
moment is known to be very near. In real life there is
always a terrible suspense in the presence of a dying
person. And even in the case of trivial happenings
which are about to take place we may be held in suspense. There is a spell of alert attention in the New
Year's Eve crowd on Broadway watching the ball of
fire on the *Times* flag pole, waiting for it to fall, to
mark the exact moment of the passing of the old year.
Expectancy is strong but is tempered with just a bit
of doubt. Our watches may not agree exactly with
the *Times* clock, and the ball may fall sooner or later
than we expected.

So in the photoplay we may for a few moments be
kept keenly on the lookout even when we know what
is going to happen. In *Intolerance* we know that rescue will come for The Boy even after he has ascended
the scaffold. We should be willing to bet our whole
fortune that the automobile will arrive with the pardon
in time. And yet until the automobile actually does
arrive we are tense with excitement. We almost forget that this is a play and that in a play the pardon

must arrive in time.   There is not a chance in a thousand that the pardon will be too late, and yet we are at palpitating attention until The Boy is safe.   Photoplays are full of effects such as this, where the spectators are in momentary suspense because of something which they know is about to happen.   In some farce a gentleman places his silk hat in a chair.   A fat lady comes in.   We know that she is going to sit down on that hat.   We rivet our eyes on her.   She does.   They always do in farces.   In some melodrama of war time we see a trans-Atlantic liner attempting to run the blockade.   A submarine emerges.   The torpedo is fired.   It will surely sink the ship.   We watch the white wake of the torpedo.   It does sink the ship.   They always do in melodrama.

"Momentary tensions of interest can easily be produced by pictures." The hack writer of photoplays can crank them out by the thousands.   But the pity of it all is that so often these momentary thrills violate the principle of unity because they have no relation to each other or to any main theme of the play.   They are mountain peaks, isolated and with no forward reach, when they should be merely curves and undulations in the road which actually leads somewhere. Therefore the scenario writer must be careful to sustain our interest in the main object of our journey through the plot, and not to get us so interested in things along the way that we forget where we are going.   If we are going to find out whether Shylock is to have his revenge or not, it would be bad art to fix our attention on the terrified faces of the sailors on Antonio's storm-tossed ships.   So in the photoplay it is bad art to put us in momentary suspense about an episode unless that momentary suspense sustains and intensifies our suspense concerning the main issue. "Therefore it is much better to keep the audience guessing as to *what* will happen, or even *what* has happened, than to have them alertly waiting for the exact moment *when* an imminent happening will come." If the audience can always tell from the beginning of an episode how it is going to end, then not even a hundred thrills of whatever intensity can ever fuse a succession of episodes into a unified, progressive, dramatic action.

Thus we have explained that one of the secrets of capturing and holding the attention of the spectator is to put him in a state of suspense concerning the events of the play. But it is also possible to put him in suspense regarding the characters in a play. The spectator may wonder what the true nature of the character will prove to be, or he may wonder whether the character will change under the influence of the happenings in the plot. One of the most fascinating problems in our social life is the problem of really understanding the true characters of our fellows. How often we hear the remarks, " I can't quite make him out," or " She is a puzzle to me." Now if in reality these uncomprehended associates are placed in circumstances where they are likely to reveal themselves more clearly, we are alertly expectant as to the result. Such means of arousing human interest can be transferred to the fictitious life of the stage or the screen. As an example of dramatic suspense with regard to character we may cite Henri Bernstein's stage play, *The Secret*. In this play the heroine brings about unhappiness on all sides. Her harmfulness consists mainly in her persistent falsehoods. We wonder why she tells these lies. Is it because she is herself mistaken? No. Is it because she seeks justifiable revenge? No. Retribution whether justifiable or not? No. Then what is the secret of her character? At the end of the play our suspense is relieved. The secret of her character is that she has a mania for mendacity. There is no purpose in her lies. She just can't help telling them. That is the kink in her character.

Telling lies would, of course, have no camera value, but acting lies would. A man may smile and smile and be a villain. But if we are sure that he is a villain we are not in suspense about his character. We are only in suspense when the play challenges us to interpret his character by his smiles, to tell what they really mean. It is obvious, therefore, that here the subtle means of suspense depends almost wholly on the actor. If the cinema composer aspires to create a character whose real nature is not to be revealed until the audience has been held in suspense for a considerable length of time, he must write for a particular performer, keeping in mind all the time the actor's powers of partly revealing and partly concealing the truth until the dramatic moment of complete unveiling.

" The gradual development of character is feasible in the photoplay, though not as easily achieved there as in the stage play or in the novel." Under given conditions human character is capable of change, of growth or decay. The process of this change, if revealed visually, can make a strong emotional appeal to the spectator. If we perceive that there is going to be a change, but cannot tell just what that change is to be, or whether it is to be permanent or not, our suspense is immediately aroused. And this tension is not relieved until the personal development has reached a certain finality.

The prime condition of an absorbed interest in dramatic character is, of course, the presence of character in the play. Many photoplays contain no characters at all; they have merely people who have not had a chance to develop personalities, that is, to become characters. If the photoplay really exhibits characters in action, this action becomes more interesting for what it signifies than for what it is. The deed becomes a finger post, interesting, not in itself, but because of what it points to. For example, in Stevenson's short story, *Markheim,* the hero commits a murder at the beginning of the story. Then, without leaving the scene of the crime, he goes through a long mental struggle trying to decide whether to escape or to surrender himself to the police. We are interested in the decision he is to make because his act will determine his character. While he is still debating the question the maid of the house comes in. He tells her to go and call the police. Here Stevenson ends the story, and it is quite proper that he should do so; because after the character has been revealed we do not care about the consequent arrest and trial, no matter how exciting this action might be. The development of character here may be contrasted with George Eliot's excellent study of moral decay in *Romola.* The hero, a bright-eyed, lovable, young Greek, begins with the noble intention of selling some jewels in order to raise money for the ransom of his foster-father, who has been enslaved by the Turks. He comes to Florence, where, having persuaded himself that his father is probably dead, or could not be easily ransomed, he yields to the temptations of pleasure and the opportunity of making a career for himself. This decision marks the beginning of a long series of actions which furnish us the spectacle of the hero's degeneration. We are alertly interested in his deeds because of what they will indicate concerning the development of his character. Perhaps he will yet change for the better. Perhaps the love of a pure woman, or the power of religion, or some other great influence will yet save him from complete moral dissolution. No. These influences work in vain. Nothing avails. He sinks into the depths, and ends his career when his foster-father strangles him to death.

While it is true that the growth of character can be more convincingly represented in the novel than in any other narrative art, yet it must be admitted that for certain plots the stage play and even the screen play can furnish adequate and vivid portrayal of personal development. "Actions sometimes speak louder than words." Recall the happenings in *Macbeth* and you see how vividly they portray the development of the hero from the man who is too full of the milk of human kindness to the man who can slay a babe or a comrade without a quiver of misgiving, and the development of his wife from the unscrupulous woman of criminal mettle to the sleep-walking victim of remorse. In such a photoplay as *The Painted Soul*, analysed in the previous chapter, the suspense of the audience is aroused as they watch the steady, subtle change in the character of the heroine.

Still another kind of dramatic suspense with regard to character is the interest in the stability of the character, that is, a kind of hope, complexed by doubt, that the character will not change. The classic example of heroic stability of character is to be found in the Greek tragedy, *Prometheus Bound.* Prometheus had bestowed the boon of fire upon men, wresting it from the gods. For this, Zeus has chained him to a rock, and afflicts him with continual pleading and mockery, and torture, and threat. Prometheus may gain his freedom by disclosing a certain secret to Zeus. We behold the spectacle of unheard of torture, and almost fear that the hero will be tempted to surrender. But his resolution is unshakable. He remains firm through the final catastrophe, when, amidst thunder and lightning, the earth yawns and engulfs him. In this thrilling play we are interested, not in the spectacular natural phenomenon, but in the character of the victim chained to the rock, and the question whether his spirit will triumph over the mighty powers arrayed against him.

It is even possible to construct a plot so that the audience rather hopes that its central figure will not change for the better. This is the nature of the suspense in Anspacher's play, *The Unchastened Woman.* The heroine is malicious and harmful to nearly every one that she comes in contact with. In the last act her husband tries efficiently to chasten her, and has almost forced her to revoke one of her most harmful statements, a revelation concerning a young woman about to be married. Curiously enough our sympathies are so placed that we hope the woman will not turn good. We are not disappointed. The husband's machinery of force breaks down, and the wife remains unchastened to the end. Somewhat the same kind of interest holds the reader of Sudermann's novel, *The Song of Songs*. In this book a woman of obviously weak moral fibre indulges in a picturesque career of social wrongdoing. She aspires rather feebly to lead a purer and nobler life, and imagines that some day and in some way her father's musical composition, " The Song of Songs," will redeem her. By the time we have read to the middle of the book we feel reasonably certain that no such redemption will ever come. Still one can never tell what a novelist might do with his characters. He might turn sentimental. Therefore we read on with alert attention to the temptations, opportunities, words, thoughts, and deeds of the heroine. She keeps on aspiring, but never redeems herself. We lay down the book satisfied with the outcome. She did not change. We did not think she would.

The average hack writer of photoplay " continuity " will not take kindly to the suggestion that spectators can be kept in a state of suspense concerning the outcome of character development. He would think you totally demented if you talked to him about the spiritual significance of physical deeds, or the use of external action to indicate inner progress. And while he pities you he will write again, this time in his seven hundredth scenario, that thrilling bit of action, almost too tense for human endurance, where the hero's motor car wins a heart breaking race against the Twentieth Century Limited. But the scenario writer who wishes to expand his powers until he commands all the possibilities of the screen must learn that many plots can be doubled in impressiveness if the emphasis is shifted from the happenings to the personalities, and if the separate acts be looked upon as separate brush strokes in the process of painting a character.

But there are still other means of keeping an audience in suspense. If it were not so it would be impossible to enjoy a photoplay more than once or to be thrilled by a photoplay with a familiar plot. We may be as familiar with the action of a plot as we are with the routine of our daily lives, and may know the characters as well as the members of our own families, and yet be kept intensely alert during a performance, wondering how the action will look when it comes, or how the play is to be interpreted this time. Not *what* but *how* is the question which occupies our attention. You may have read the story of *Carmen,* may have seen it as a stage play, may have attended the opera, and yet may be kept in suspense from beginning to end of the Lasky *Carmen* because you wonder how your favourite scenes will look on the screen. And then you may go eagerly to see the Fox *Carmen* because you wonder how Theda Bara is going to interpret the rôle in which Geraldine Farrar has just been fascinating you. In the case of original plays which we have not yet seen it happens often that some talkative initiate tells us in general what the action is and how the plot ends. Still we may attend that play with a feeling of suspense as to how the known action will be treated. The majority of us who saw the first performance of Lord Dunsany's little play *The Gods of the Mountain* knew already from reading the play that at the end the true gods would turn the imposters, seven beggars, into stone. Yet we followed the play with steady interest, especially toward the end, because we wondered just how that transformation was to be done. This kind of suspense might be termed treatment suspense, to distinguish it from action suspense and character suspense.

The photoplay may even have author suspense, if we may coin another expression. When the art of the photoplay has become a little older, when the cinema composers have come into their full expression, so that their various individualities and styles can be recognized by the public, we may have a new kind of suspense in the motion picture theatre. We may find ourselves in an alert expectancy, looking for manifestations of the author's self-expression in style as the story proceeds from point to point. "Individualities of style have long been present in stage drama." When we see or read a play by Shakespeare we are alert for evidences of the author's characteristic touch, as well as for developments in action or character. One of these touches is the poetic passage. We know that at any moment and on the slightest provocation Shakespeare is likely to burst into a flight of poetry, and we look forward to it as we would to a characteristic phrase in music. When we see or read a play by Shaw we experience a somewhat similar suspense with regard to the author's self-expression. We know that at any moment Shaw is likely to say something paradoxical, or shocking, or wittily stimulating, and we are alertly attentive lest we miss the point. What is true of words will be true of motion pictures; the medium reveals the personality of the artist. Under more ideal conditions in the future the cinema composer will direct or supervise his own production, and his composition will then reach the spectators intact and bearing the stamp of the author's personality.

We have thus shown specifically the manysided nature of suspense, the essential element in dramatic appeal. We have shown that audiences may be kept in suspense regarding the individuality of the author or of the performer, regarding the nature or development of the character, and regarding the happenings of the past and of the future. Regarding all these things suspense can be sustained, but suspense must be aroused before it can be sustained. In the case of interest in the author or of the performer suspense springs from our past experience, from our previous acquaintance with their work. But in the case of the characters or happenings of a play we begin with our emotions calm and our minds in a state of indifference or neutrality. This neutrality of attitude must be broken at the beginning of the play; for if we have no particular sympathy for any of the characters we will, of course, not care what happens to them, and therefore will never be in suspense at all. How to make the spectators sympathize with some, if not all, of his characters in a photoplay is one of the important problems of the cinema composer.

In the chapter on the " Psychology of the Cinema Audience " we used the term " social emotion " to include all our personal interest in the fictitious characters on the screen. We may have a social attitude toward them, whether of love or hate, admiration or contempt, pity or scorn, as we would if they were actually our fellow citizens in real life. And this social emotion determines our concern about what happens to them. We look forward to punishment for those we hate, and happiness for those we love; but we do not in the least care what happens to those who have in no way stirred our emotions or attracted our attention.

The social emotion must be established early in the play, because, unless suspense starts early, the play will not capture the audience. This means that the cinema composer will have to establish a friendship or an enmity within a few minutes of action. There must be love or hate at first sight. If the people on the screen, perfect strangers to us, could come down into the audience to meet us personally it would not be difficult for us to become acquainted. But they cannot come in contact with us; they do not even know of our existence. They are more remote than the passers-by of a busy street whom we idly watch from our window.

But there is a dramatic device, a device which dramatists have known for three thousand years, by which almost instantaneously our sympathies can be enlisted and our suspense aroused. It is the human struggle. Let any two strangers in the street start a fight and we soon cease to be idle watchers. We soon sympathize with one as against the other. We may perhaps maintain neutrality of the hand, but we cannot possibly maintain a neutrality of the heart. You never yet saw a fight or struggle or conflict or game in which you did not take sides in the contention. And as soon as you had taken a side in the issue you were in suspense until the struggle ended. The dramatist, therefore, after focalizing his interest on some one character in the play, places that character in conflict with some one else, a revengeful enemy, an unscrupulous rival, a narrow-minded parent, a scornful lady, or any one of the thousand antagonists that may cross our pursuit of happiness in life.   The antagonist need not always be a person.   It may be poverty or hunger or cold.   It may be appetite or temptation or disease. It may be jealousy or suspicion or superstition.   It may be injustice or iniquity or adverse opinion.   The chief character may struggle with himself, with his past, with circumstance, or with fate.   But as surely as there is a dramatic struggle, and the stakes are worth fighting for, the spectators will remain in the theatre until they know who wins the fight.

Some of the technical principles in handling a dramatic conflict are often ignored or violated by the untrained writer.   He does not balance the struggle well, thereby making the outcome too easily foreseen.   Or he attracts our sympathy to the wrong combatant.   Or, so frequently in the photoplay, he makes the conflict a mere episode in the action instead of making it the play itself.   If the duel or the fist fight or the assault or the hair pulling contest or the automobile-train race is merely an incident of the larger, sustained struggle which is fundamental in the play, well and good.   But if this conflict is a thrilling episode which attracts attention to itself without adding to the play as a whole, the dramatic emphasis is bad; and, furthermore, the suspense of the spectator is not maintained except during the episode.   Besides, even in the motion picture play it is not always necessary that a dramatic conflict lead to a personal combat between the strugglers.   Breaking a man's jaw is only one of the many visible acts which reveal your hatred of him.   The photoplaywright who is aspiring to improve his art will learn a valuable lesson in the pictorial presentation of drama if he makes a list of all the photoplays in which the struggle is clearly set forth without the resort to a physical combat.

Another objection to the brief fight or the race is that the suspense is relieved too soon. No spectator would want a prize fight to last only one round, or a foot ball game only five minutes, or a presidential campaign only one week. "So in the photoplay suspense should come early and last long." A big question should be asked early in the play and the answer should be withheld from the audience until the end of the play. This wait between the question and the answer is what the spectator is paying for. If there is no wait there is no dramatic appeal. What would have happened to the dramatic values if Antonio had discovered the flaw in Shylock's bond during the second act, or if Romeo and Juliet had committed suicide in the balcony scene, or if Oswald had learned the truth about his father before the end of the first act? Such actions would be probable enough, would, in fact, bear a strong resemblance to real life, but would obviously tend to frustrate the steady dramatic appeal which the present arrangement of the action produces.

One of the trade marks of the photoplay plot which has been concocted over night is the presence of theatrical effects which have not been led up to by any suspense whatsoever, of emphatic answers to questions that no one has ever asked. Even in the hands of the skilled playwright the dramatic surprise proves unsatisfactory to the audience. We mean the complete surprise. The audience does not resent partial surprises, unforeseen details in the development of the action, but it looks upon the complete surprise as a shock. The cinema composer should not shoot his thunderbolt out of a clear sky. He should prepare for the effect by letting the wind go down and the thunder heads gather in the West.

During the greater part of the play the spectator wants to be kept in suspense, pays for it, and demands it. He would be thoroughly disappointed if it were relieved too soon. But there comes a time in every plot when the spectator suddenly wants the suspense relieved, and he would be equally disappointed if that relief did not come. The end must be something more than a logical result. It must satisfy the heart as well as the mind. It must be emotionally satisfactory. We must feel that dramatic justice has been rendered, and go home with a moral approval of the solution of the dramatic conflict. These principles seem almost too obvious to be enunciated. And yet the vast majority of photoplays at present exhibited violate them constantly, especially in the case of the sentimentally happy ending. In the cheap, inartistic photoplay the vampire finds her haven in the arms of her devoted husband, the voluptuary discovers that the woman he raped is his own wife, and the murderer one fine morning receives a letter from his victim, who didn't die after all. It does not require much philosophy to see that these finishing touches are positively immoral, if they are taken seriously; if they are not taken seriously they are merely vulgar stupidities. A perfect play is by illusion a section of life, and the spectator wants to feel that, on the whole, the rewards of life are not accidental but deserved. The ending of a play may be sad and yet may be emotionally satisfactory. *Carmen* is a case in point. The outcome of the dramatic action is that Don Jose kills Carmen and then himself. It is sad, but somehow we feel that it is right. Our mood is in the same high key as the play. It seems to us that Carmen deserved to die; and that without her, life was not worth while to Don Jose. As for Escamillo, the toreador, well, perhaps he will find some other señorita no less sweet than Carmen.

If the progression of pictured actions has succeeded in arousing the spectator's suspense and has relieved that suspense in an emotionally satisfactory way we may say of such a cinematic composition that it has great dramatic appeal. The test of this plot quality is an emotional test. An intellectual test must also be applied to a plot before we can say whether its construction approaches the perfection demanded of high art. Let us see in the next chapter just how this critical test may be satisfied in a well-constructed play.

CHAPTER XIII

THE CONSTRUCTION OF A PLOT

IN the chapters on pictorial composition we have shown that pictures, whether static or in motion, are most satisfactory to the spectator when they are constructed according to the principles of unity, balance, emphasis, and rhythm. The same principles of construction must obtain in the plot as a whole. The plot as such must contain a single, organized movement from a starting point to a stopping point. It must have a satisfactory balance between cause and effect, between action and consequence, between complication and solution. It must emphasize suspense at certain times, accelerating the action toward a crisis or the climax and retarding it away from such a period. And it must carry the attention of the spectator in a rhythmical line from the mental and emotional repose at the beginning of the play, through the intense mental alertness and emotional stir at the climax, down to the mental and emotional repose at the end of the play. These are the tests which the spectator applies consciously or unconsciously to the finished play; and these are the tests which the cinema composer must apply deliberately to his play while it is still in the making.

In order to possess unity a play must have all its ingredients, no matter how diverse they seem to be organized into a single totality. It must be, not a part, but a whole, a complete thing. It must start somewhere, try to get somewhere, and get there; or, as Aristotle said more than two thousand years ago, it must have a beginning, a middle, and an end.

The problem of so constructing a play that it shall have definite totality, complete unity, involves, but does not depend upon, the number of units in that play. A stage play of five separate acts may have perfect unity, while a play of a single act may show a tendency to fall apart into incoherent elements. It must be remembered here that by a unit in a play we mean that part of the action which the spectator is allowed to perceive with uninterrupted attention. In spoken drama a unit is that part of the play which comes between the rise and fall of the curtain. During that unit the attention is held, and between such units it is given a recess and may turn to other things. In the photoplay the unit is any continuous projection on the screen. It ends when the projection stops for any length of time sufficient for us to rest our eyes and talk with our companions about the play or about other things.

"This difference between the units of attention in a photoplay and in a stage drama has not always been grasped by scenario writers, who have looked on the reel (a thousand feet of film) as the unit of attention." A reel would, of course, be a unit of attention only when the showing of that reel was followed by a fairly long intermission before the showing of the next reel, thus permitting the spectator to take his attention off the screen and turn it to something else. But it must be observed that under present conditions of exhibition in most theatres several reels are shown continuously without any intermission. The favourite length for serious photoplays is five reels, which requires the uninterrupted attention of the spectator for a whole hour. Therefore a five reel photoplay is at present to be looked upon as a one part composition. A six reel photoplay would also be shown as a one part composition. This does not mean, however, that a ten or twelve reel photoplay must be shown as a two part composition. It is true that such a division is at present usually made by the exhibitor, but it is not true that the division into two parts gives the best impression of unity in the whole play. On the contrary, it is difficult to compose two parts, especially if they be equal in size and significance, into one coherent whole. This difficulty confronts the painter or sculptor who is to combine two equal figures into one artistic effect, and this difficulty confronts the builder of plots for the stage or for the screen who is asked to divide his plots into two equal parts. Therefore, if the photoplay is more than, say, an hour and a half in length it would be better to divide it into three or more parts, not necessarily equal in length.

When we test a plot for unity of structure we see that there are two main systems of dramatic development, resulting in two different types of plot, which we shall call the " bead-string plot " and the " cable plot." In the bead-string plot a series of actions are so strung together that, although they are in a succession they are not logically connected, and their order can be changed or any one action can be removed, without materially affecting the meaning of the play. In the cable plot the various dramatic elements are like strands woven tightly about each other so that no single strand could be removed without weakening the plot.

The bead-string plot is often used for farces and sometimes for serious plays. An example of the use in farce is *One A. M.,* a "vehicle" for Charlie Chaplin. The drunken Charlie has been given a key to a friend's house and told that he may spend the night there. He enters via the window, stepping into a bowl of gold fish. Then he finds the key, goes out through the window, and enters properly through the door. Because of unstable equilibrium he skates about over the waxed floor, finally landing between a tiger rug and a wild cat rug, which alternately scare him out of his wits. He gets up and leans on a table only to find that it mysteriously swings around. He attempts to use a selzer bottle, with the usual effect. He attempts to go upstairs, but is so frightened by a stuffed ostrich that he rolls down the balustrade, incidentally landing right in front of a whiskey bottle. He tries the stairs vaguely again, and, losing his balance at the top, grasps the "runner" which pulls loose and wraps itself around him as he rolls down. He tries the pair of stairs at the other side of the room, but is struck by the huge, swinging pendulum of a clock, and again rolls down, embracing a stuffed bear as he makes the descent. He finally ascends to the upper landing via a coat tree, and, after much trouble with a patent door, lies down in a folding bed, which, of course, collapses upon him. After much more farcical business with the bed he goes to the bath room and accidentally turns on the shower, beneath which he is standing. He finally lies down in the bath tub to sleep, protected from the cold by the bath mat. A plot like this needs no further comment in a chapter on dramatic construction.

And yet even a bead-string plot may have a kind of unity other than unity of time or place.   The beads may be graduated in size, so that each bead is followed by a larger one, which could not be omitted or misplaced without spoiling the organized progression. This may be illustrated in Maeterlinck's *The Blue Bird,* which has been discussed in the chapter on symbolism.   Two children search for the blue bird of happiness in five different places, arranged in the following order: The Land of Memory, The Palace of Night, The Forest, The Graveyard, and the Kingdom of the Future.   There is a kind of logical order here which becomes more evident as one studies the play.   Yet even here the sections might be separated, as was shown by the fact that Maeterlinck himself wrote an additional act, which he called " The Palace of Happiness," and placed between The Forest and The Graveyard.   Perhaps the best that can be said about the bead-string plot after all is that it is not difficult to construct.

In the cable plot the various motives and forces exist not consecutively but side by side, touch, and are twisted firmly about, each other.   Such a plot is *The Merchant of Venice.*   Let us name the dramatic elements in the order in which we are informed of them in the play.   Bassanio's friendship with Antonio, his love for Portia, his need of money, Portia's wealth, Antonio's ships at sea, his generosity, the love-lottery of the caskets, Portia's wit, Shylock's hatred of Antonio, the pound-of-flesh bond, the two clowns, Jessica's elopement, the wedding rings, the disguise of Portia and Nerissa.   These are the essential ingredients of the play.   But it will be observed that each ingredient appears, not merely once, like a bead on a string, but more continuously, paralleling itself with other ingredients, touching them, now above now below, winding about them, stretching forward through the plot like strands in a cable. The love-lottery (though not the love making) and the clowns are lost sight of early; they are short strands. But the other strands reach to the very end of the play. It is more difficult to construct a cable plot than a bead-string plot, because it is more difficult to manage several motives and forces simultaneously than to manage them one at a time. But the cable plot when finished has more organic unity, more firmness and strength than the bead-string plot.

But the whole of any plot, no matter of what pattern, whether long or short, whether exhibited without intermission or with two, three, or more intermissions, consists naturally of three parts. The action reaches a point, even though the spectator may not be aware of it, where the beginning ends, and another point where the end begins; between these two points extends what Aristotle called the middle. Instead of the terms beginning, middle, and end we prefer to substitute the terms premise, complication, and solution. Any plot, whether simple or involved, direct or devious, bare or decorated, long or short, old or new, must be built on the frame work premise-complication-solution. And no plot maker can say that he has a plot until he has arranged his characters and actions firmly into that framework, thus organizing all his parts into a complete unity.

The premise is the point of departure which contains the initial causes, the basic conditions of complication.

In *Romeo and Juliet* the premise represents two families in a feud and shows how the son in one family
falls in love with the daughter in the other. When
the audience has received so much of the story it has
the basis for all the ensuing tragedy. In *The Merchant of Venice* the premise is the signing of the contract to the effect that if the borrower cannot repay the
stated sum within three months the lender may cut
out a pound of flesh from any part of the borrower's
body. The audience realize clearly the danger in such
a contract and can guess at the complication to which
it leads. In *Macbeth* the premise informs the audience that Macbeth wants to become king, that his wife
endorses the ambition and is determined to see it realized even if it should become necessary to murder the
reigning monarch, and that the fated monarch is on
his way to Macbeth's home for a visit. Here the
premise ends. The play can go no farther without
leading us into the complication. In the premise of
Wilde's *Lady Windermere's Fan* we get the wife's
discovery that her husband has been paying out large
sums of money to some mysterious woman, the husband's defence of his action, and his demand that the
woman be invited to their party that evening, the wife's
reply that she will disgrace the strange woman if she
comes, the husband's insistence, and his aside to the
audience, " I dare not tell here who this woman really
is." At the beginning of Pinero's *The Second Mrs.
Tanqueray* we learn that Tanqueray is about to marry
a woman of notorious past, saying " I'll prove to you
that it's possible to rear a life of happiness, of good
repute, on a miserable foundation." The premise of
the play is complete when we learn that his young

daughter, Ellean, has decided to come home to be his companion.

In every one of the cases cited the premise is promising, pointing forward, and therefore truly a part of an organized progression. It contains immediate suggestion of possible complication. It grips the attention of the spectator and induces him to speculate on the entanglements which are likely to follow. This is the function of the premise, to arouse the suspense of the spectator, and at the same time to serve as the foundation upon which the structure of the play proper is to be reared. First the plot builder must make sure that his premise will arouse suspense. It is not enough merely to introduce the characters of his play in one or more interesting settings. It is not enough merely to show these characters talking, signing papers, eating dinner, or kissing. Whatever the characters are and whatever they do, they must produce a situation.

Situation! What is a dramatic situation? We have looked in books but have not yet found a satisfactory definition of the term. Therefore we will have to make one of our own. A situation is an action or state of affairs which arouses suspense in the mind of the participant or of the spectator. Suspense is the key word. And suspense, as we have shown in the preceding chapter, always takes the form of some question for which the answer is always more or less remotely out of reach. Antonio's borrowing money of Shylock is an action, but it does not become a situation until the pound-of-flesh clause has been put into the contract. This situation arouses some suspense in the mind of Shylock and a great deal more in the mind of the spectator. The existence of a family feud is a state of affairs, but it does not arouse any particular suspense until it is involved with the love affair of Romeo and Juliet.   Then comes to hero, heroine, and all of the spectators the question " Now what is to be done? "   The premise, therefore, should include an initial situation which starts the main suspense of the play, the suspense which is not to be relieved until the solution of the play.

The beginning of a play should grip the attention, the mental interest, of the spectator, but it should not be allowed to appeal too strongly to his emotions. The spectator enjoys a play most when he is allowed to approach and enter it with unprejudiced, emotionally neutral, mind, and then is allowed to deepen his sympathies for the central characters in their dramatic difficulties.   He does not want to feel utter contempt and hatred for Shylock from the very beginning, for then the remainder of the play will lack emotional progress and will seem weak and anticlimactic by contrast with the beginning.   The law of emphasis, or accelerating progression applies to the emotions of the spectator as well as to his mental interest in the development of the action.   Shakespeare, recognizing this law, has introduced Shylock in such a way that the audience cannot at first tell whether he is a victim or a villain.   The Jew recounts a long list of injuries received at the hands of Antonio and finishes with the statement that despite these injuries he will lend Antonio the money if he will set his seal to the unusual bond.   But this bond is suggested only in a merry sport, he says, and the exaction of the forfeiture would bring him no gain.   It is only the Christians, he says, whose own hard dealings makes them suspect the motives of others. All this comes in the premise of the play. But as the action progresses, the spectator learns that Shylock really expects to cut the heart out of Antonio, a resolution from which he cannot be swerved by pleadings for mercy or by offers of many times the amount of money involved in the bond. And the spectator's emotions are gradually heightened by this discovery of the real nature of the villain. What is true of *The Merchant of Venice* should be true of all plays. " The premise should rouse the suspense of the spectator without inducing his prejudice for or against any character in the play."

Besides arousing suspense the premise should serve as an adequate foundation for the ensuing complication of the plot. The law of balance demands that the premise must be logically sufficient for the complication. The premise must contain the main causes of which the complication contains the main effects. If the initial causes are too slight or too great in proportion to the effects, the result will be an unbalanced, unconvincing plot, unconvincing to the spectator even before he has had time to analyse the lack of logical balance. Thus if Antonio had never offended Shylock, and if Shylock had not insisted on the fatal clause in the bond, it would have been dramatically unconvincing to represent the Jew as ready to kill the Christian on the day of the trial. Thus also if Macbeth had not been shown as insanely desirous of kingship, and his wife had not urged him to regicide, the murder of Duncan would have come as a shock to the audience, a violent improbability in no way dramatically convincing. The plot maker must satisfy himself that his premise is a good preparation for the rest of the play, that it will

serve as a logically solid foundation for the main complication, that the causes balance with the effects.

Dramatic convincingness involves the question of
probability. The probability of a dramatic premise
has two phases; first, the probability that such initial
conditions exist, and, second, the probability that such
initial conditions will lead to dramatic complication.
In all the examples above given it is extremely probable that the given conditions, if they existed, would
lead to the given complication.   But the existence of
the given initial conditions is not in every case probable. It is more probable that Romeo and Juliet
should fall in love than that an experienced merchant
should sign a note to the effect that if he could not
meet the note he would let the lender cut out a pound
of his flesh. Another play of Shakespeare's, *The
Comedy of Errors,* illustrates a still greater improbability in the existence of the initial conditions.   The
premise of this comedy tells us that a pair of twins,
boys of noble birth, were separated in a shipwreck and
washed to shores of separate countries, where they
grew up, each ignorant of his brother's existence.   In
the same shipwreck a pair of twins, slave boys, were
also separated and washed to the same separate shores
as the noble boys, each ignorant of his brother's existence, and each becoming the servant of the noble boy
washed to the same shore.   The comedy begins when
noble A with slave B accidentally comes to the village
where noble A', now married, lives with slave B'.   It
can be seen at once that the probability of complication
is extremely great.   The wife will make love to, or
upbraid, A instead of A'; she will punish B for not car-
rying out orders given to B'; in the same way the two

masters will each mistake the other's slave for his own, and the two slaves will carry messages each to the wrong master; the villagers will confuse the two nobles in social or business matters, until the play becomes a mystic maze of errors. Of course, the solution is possible at any moment of the play by simply letting one twin meet his brother or by letting some one else see the twins simultaneously. But are the initial conditions of this play probable? Certainly not.

Yet the plot maker will find upon experimentation that more or less improbability in the assumptions of the premise will insure great probability of complication. In the case of *The Comedy of Errors* the amount of mistaken identity would have been greatly reduced if the twin slaves had been omitted from the story, and would have shrunk to a minimum if one of the nobles had known of his brother's existence in the same village. Such tameness of action the spectators would not like; they prefer to accept the given premise, improbable as it is, for the sake of the resulting comedy. It is as though an agreement had been struck between the audience and the playwright to the effect that they will not question his causes, providing he will give them sufficiently amusing or interesting effects. The play maker of today or tomorrow will find his audience equally generous, equally willing to play the game of make-believe. They will pretend that the premises are true, providing the sequels are consistently interesting. In fact, if the complication is sufficiently enthralling they will soon forget that the premise was not true. The question of just how much improbability the audience will accept at the beginning must be answered by each writer for himself. It depends partly on the type of plot he is constructing.   In farce or melodrama considerable improbability is permitted and even desired.   In a serious dramatic interpretation of contemporary conditions it is better to keep as close as possible to life as it really is.

"The fact that a photoplay is a play in pictures and not in words involves a special problem of arrangement. The cinema composer must select and arrange his pictures so that he may satisfy the psychological demand for accelerating progression toward some point of emphasis.   This means that the pictures which are most appealing and impressive either in subject or pictorial composition may not appear during the premise of the play.   To place the pictorial climax at the beginning would be as fatal to the play as to place the plot climax there.   Throughout the remainder of the play the eye would be displeased because the pictorial beauty was not up to the standard set at the beginning.   We do not mean to imply that the poorest picture of a set should be selected for the beginning of a play.   It is always well to make a good impression at the beginning." But we do mean that however beautiful the pictures are at the beginning they should become still more beautiful as the play progresses. The responsibility for the picture arrangement in a photoplay is borne partly by the scenario writer, who specifies and describes the pictures he wants, but more largely by the director, who directs the actual taking of the pictures.   It surely is no difficult task to arrange beautiful pictures in a climactic order, or at least in an order which shall not be anticlimactic.   Suppose, for example, a number of scenes are to be taken on the picturesque lawn in front of some colonial mansion.

Now it is a familiar fact that a country estate is not equally beautiful from all angles. Therefore it seems obvious that the best view of the setting should be reserved for the scene which is to come last in the play, providing, of course, that such arrangement in no way interfered with the dramatic emphasis of the plot. This principle of cinematic composition should be applied throughout the play so that the spectator might perceive ever increasing beauty of picture at the same time that he experiences heightening suspense concerning the dramatic action. "It is advisable, therefore, to make the premise of the photoplay pictorially calm or neutral, neither noticeably good nor noticeably bad."

''The length of the premise in proportion to the other two sections of the plot must be greater in the photoplay than in the stage play, because it takes longer for the devices of pantomime and screen to present the initial situation so clearly that it may be easily grasped by the spectator and remembered by him throughout the play.'' On the stage characters may be introduced and identified in groups of five or six at a time. On the screen they must be introduced singly or in groups of two or three lest the spectator be confused and attach the names to the wrong characters." Also, without dialog, it takes longer for the character to reveal enough of his nature to give the spectator sufficient basis for judging the subsequent action, this, of course, providing the character has any nature to reveal. And while the spectator is becoming acquainted with the characters he must be clearly informed as to their dramatic relations to each other." For example, if a man and a woman are pictured together it should be made clear as soon as possible whether they are brother and sister, man and wife, sweethearts, business associates, or dance partners. A kiss is not reliable evidence; therefore the scenario writer who is in a hurry is likely to resort to a bit of dialog to be thrown on the screen. As critics we object to words in a picture play, yet we must admit that if words have to be used they are more to be tolerated in the premise of the play than anywhere else. But better still would be to make the action self-explanatory.

When does the first section of the play, the premise, end? It ends when the main suspense of the play has been aroused in the minds of the audience. It ends when the spectators begin to wonder whether Romeo and Juliet can ever be happily married under the circumstances; whether Shylock will ever have occasion to get that pound of flesh; whether Macbeth will kill the king who is to be his guest; whether Lady Windermere really will strike Mrs. Erlynne with her fan; how the pure minded young Ellean will get along with her stepmother, the second Mrs. Tanqueray.

"The end of the premise in a spoken drama usually coincides with the end of the first act or with the end of one of the early scenes in the play, and is therefore marked by the dropping of the curtain and followed by an intermission." This intermission serves other purposes besides providing for the lapse of time and the change of scenery. It gives the spectator a chance to relax his attention, lest he grow weary of seeing and hearing. It provides the downward curve in the rhythmical line of attention. And yet, the spectator while resting his senses may ponder over the premise of the play, he may recall it until it becomes firmly established in his mind. On the other hand, the intermission may in some cases serve to increase suspense. It may be the dramatic pause which makes the spectator only the more eager for the continuation of the story.   A similar use of the dramatic pause is seen in the serial fiction of magazines, where the story breaks off at some strategic point, to be continued in the next number.   But in the usual five reel photoplay, as in the one act stage play, there can be no intermission at the end of the premise; at least, there can be no suspension of the show.

'"Yet the photoplay has already developed a device to which all of the functions of the stage intermission may be transferred." That device, known in the studios as the " cut-back," is the instantaneous shifting from one plot or set of actions to another parallel plot or set of actions.   The " cut-back " may be seen skilfully used in the plays directed by Mr. Griffith, especially in *Intolerance*.   The striking originality of *Intolerance* consists in the fact that it tells four parallel stories from four different periods of history.   They are a story of ancient Babylon, the story of Christ, a story of the Huguenots, and a story of contemporary American life.   Shakespeare often paralleled several plots in one play, but they were never laid in different periods of history.   The characters in the sub-plot could always meet, or communicate with, the characters in the main plot.   Mr. Griffith uses the " cut-back " to allow for the change of scene or lapse of time in any one story, and to heighten the suspense of the spectator.   He may also use it in the future, if he has not done so in the past, to rest the eye of the spectator; because in the photoplay, as in real life, the change of scene and activity may serve the purpose of a rest.   Thus, when he has told us enough of the Babylonian story to rouse our interest in it, he flashes to the story of American life; and when he has presented the premise of that story, he flashes back to Babylon, or to the beginning of the story of the Huguenots. Many of those who saw *Intolerance* declare that the " cut-back " was used too much, and that the show was very exhausting to the attention.   Such criticisms contain valuable lessons for the cinema composer.   He may learn from the abuse of a device as well as from its successful use.   It is certain that no one should attempt to tell four stories in a short photoplay.   But it would be possible to tell two stories in a five reel photoplay, providing they were different enough and one were clearly subsidiary to the other.   A tragic story of criminals in contemporary life might, for example, be contrasted with a fairy story, or a whimsical, charming story of innocent childhood, so that a change from one to the other would serve all the purposes of the stage intermission.   But whether the end of the premise is marked by an intermission or a " cut-back " it comes at the point where the main suspense has been aroused.¶ And where the premise ends the complication begins. ¶

The complication, as we use the term in this chapter, comprises the main development of the plot from the premise to the point where the solution begins.   It includes the crises and the climax of the plot.   Progressing through the crises to the climax it raises suspense to its highest pitch and stirs the emotions to their profoundest depths.   Before we go any farther in this discussion we must define the terms crisis and climax. Here again we prefer our own definition to any that have been found in previous treatises of dramatic technique. Crisis is that point or portion of the plot where conflicting interests or desires meet and demand immediate adjustment. There must be a conflict, and there must be a demand for immediate adjustment. The time which intervenes between the demand and the adjustment contains intense suspense. If there is only a struggle with no necessity for immediate decision the state of affairs may be called a situation, but not a crisis. It would come under the definition of situation which we have already given. Climax is the most intense crisis of which any given plot is capable. Thus Lady Windermere's discovery that her husband has been paying large sums of money to Mrs. Erlynne, and is determined to invite her to the party is a situation. It becomes a stronger situation when Lady Windermere says she will strike the woman across the face with her fan. But the situation does not reach a crisis until the next act during the party, at the moment when Mrs. Erlynne has just been announced. Up to that point the conflicting interests of husband and wife have remained unsettled. But now immediate adjustment is demanded, the matter must be settled without a moment's delay. Will the hostess carry out her threat, offend her husband, and make a scene at the party, or will she swallow her pride, forget her grievance, and greet the woman graciously? Mrs. Erlynne stands in the doorway, so magnificent, appealing, and hypnotic that the hostess drops her fan to the floor. That crisis is over. Thus, too, in the *Merchant of Venice* the situation produced by Antonio's signing of the bond does not develop into a crisis until the moment when the audience hears Bas-

sanio read Antonio's letter to the effect that all his
ships have been lost and that his life is forfeit to the
Jew. There is now an immediate demand for the
adjustment of conflicting interests and desires. And
Bassanio and Portia proceed without delay to make
that adjustment. But time intervenes between the demand and the adjustment, and before the crisis is over
the highest suspense of the play has been developed.
Consequently this crisis is the climax of the play. We
have here given two examples of dramatic crises, one
long and one short. The crisis referred to in *Lady
Windermere's Fan* lasts only a minute, while that of
The Merchant of Venice lasts from Act III, Scene 2,
to Act IV, Scene 1. It will be seen that we use the
word climax, the Greek word for ladder, in its original
meaning. The ladder, or climax, by which we mount
to the dramatic heights of *The Merchant of Venice*
extends from the point where Bassanio reads Antonio's
letter to the point where Portia says, " Tarry a little,
there is something else."

Dramatic climax and crises thus defined are con-
tained only in what we have called the complication of
the play. The complication may also contain situations, and incidents, that is, developing actions which,
unlike situation, have no inherent suspense. And all
of these elements, while logical effects of what has
preceded, may become logical causes of what is to follow. It is in this inevitable transition from initial
causes to immediate effects to further and ultimate
effects that genuine dramatic movement is exhibited.
No rioting mob, no charging brigade, no speeding train
or motor car, no cyclone, no physical movement of any
kind can become dramatic movement unless it becomes

an organic element in the irresistible march of cause and effect, of conditions, incidents, situations, crises, and climax.

This insistent urge toward the dramatic goal must satisfy the demand of unity by furnishing effects from all the causes, and causes for all the effects. And it must satisfy the demand of convincingness by establishing a natural balance between the causes and effects. As the dramatic premise must be sufficient for the complication, so the complication must be sufficient for the premise. It must not be inferior to what the audience has been led to expect. In *The Merchant of Venice* it would be ridiculous for Shylock to say at the trial scene, " Give me the money. I have punished the poor fellow enough. Besides I would not soil my hands with his filthy blood." And, whether it were ridiculous or not, it would not be satisfactory to the audience. Nor would the audience at an exhibition of *Macbeth* be satisfied if after the dramatic preparation for the murder Macbeth came smilingly to his wife with the words, " Dearest comrade, God has blessed our desires. We will not have to slay Duncan, after all. I have just been informed by his physician that he has tuberculosis. His days are numbered." Such anti-climactic or sub-dramatic effects are frequently seen on the screen; and they cannot be justified by the explanation that they are life-like and full of optimism because they depict the happy turns that the involved affairs of men may take. " Drama is not life. It is a unified, well-balanced re-arrangement of life for the purpose of satisfying an audience." If the audience has been keyed up by the announcement that it will probably see a tiger, it will not be pleased to see only a cat, even though a cat is more life-like and re-assuring than a tiger.

On the other hand, we do not want a tiger to saunter in toward the bowl of milk we have just set out for the cat.   He is an unmotivated effect at that time, and would undoubtedly interrupt evening prayers.   So in drama an effect so large and violent that it is entirely out of proportion to the cause established as a preparation for it, would undoubtedly terminate the play-goers' devotion to that play as a serious piece of art. The lack of balance between cause and effect constitutes the melodrama of the " movies," where men are shot without being sufficiently hated, and come back to life though they have been sufficiently shot; where villains are struck by lightning while on their way to the post-office, and heroes go through years of military hell by land and sea and sky without losing a button or a swagger; where houses are burned without being set fire to, and heroines are set fire to without even being burned; and where tragic beginnings turn out to be only dreams, while happy endings come to those who had not even dreamed of such things.

Of all melodramatic effects the coincidence is the worst because it has no cause whatever.   It is as unnatural as the thunderbolt out of the clear sky.   Furthermore, the audience dislikes a coincidence not only because it is improbable but also because, coming as a shock, it robs them of the joy of dramatic expectation.   Suspense is the blending of the expected with the unexpected, and it is best relieved when the expected comes in the unexpected way.   It was to be expected, for example, that the second Mrs. Tanqueray, who has been much to many men, would have friction with the neighbours and with her pure-minded step-daughter, Ellean; but it was not foreseen that Ellean would come home with the news that she was engaged to a young man who turns out to be a former lover of the step-mother. The audience is impressed but not shocked by this dramatic climax, because they remember from the premise of the play the germs of this bitter fruitage.

But is there not such a thing as good melodrama? There is, if by " good melodrama " you mean drama in a high key, drama in broad strokes and bright colours. But such drama is not unconvincing, because the tremendous complications are balanced by tremendous causes. Values are high because contrasts are sharp, the black of sin against the white of purity, the red of passion against the green of jealousy, the heaven-high ambition against the hell-deep revenge. Such drama in high key has always been popular, and may be good art. If the cinema composer is ambitious to produce " good melodrama " he will find worthy examples in Goethe's *Faust,* in Shakespeare's *Othello,* in Marlowe's *Tamburlaine,* and in Sophocles's *Œdipus Rex.* Melodrama of the screen may be good if it is done in the mood of these plays and according to the methods of their authors. There must be balance between meaning and movement, between throbbing motives and thrilling effects. Because without this balance all spectacle and catastrophe remain undramatized. Undramatized fire and flood, explosion of mines, catapulting automobiles, thousands of men and horses dashing over miles of landscape are to be classified with the circus but not with drama.

¶ To be convincing, therefore, a play must have logical balance. ¶ But it must be impressive as well as convincing. The spectator demands that the action shall move faster and faster towards the places of emphasis, to the crises and higher still to the climax. If the initial situation urges toward the climax, the initial situation plus the first crisis should urge still harder toward the climax. This demand for cumulating interest and heightening attention is instinctive with the spectator. Even a child would be displeased by a play which had the climax at the beginning. To that child the play would be a weak thing without emphasis. But a play will have emphasis if it moves forward with accelerating tempo, with ever heightening suspense, with ever deepening emotions, with pictures ever more beautiful or more impressive until the end of the climax is reached. Thus in *The Merchant of Venice* the main suspense begins when Antonio signs the bond; it rises higher when we learn that the ships have been lost and the bond is forfeit; it rises still higher when we hear Shylock insisting on his bond; and it is highest of all at the scene when, after Shylock has refused settlement, the disguised Portia says, "A pound of that same merchant's flesh is thine. The court awards it, and the law doth give it." Meanwhile the emotions of the spectator have been deepening. He has felt gradually more admiration for Portia, more pity for Antonio, more contempt for Shylock.

This accelerating progression of suspense and emotion should be emphasized if possible by an accelerating progression of the pictorial values in the play. That is, the pictures should gradually become more beautiful, more impressive as they progress towards

the climax of the play.   This should be so because the
sequence of pictures is the language in which the photoplay expresses itself, as the sequence of words is
the language in which stage drama expresses itself.
In the masterpieces of stage drama the dialog always
is most incisive, most impressive, most memorable at
the beginning or end of a crisis or climax,   This emphasis is due partly to the content of the sentences
spoken and partly to their literary form.   Thus in the
photoplay the crises or climax of the drama should
coincide with the most striking pantomime, the most
impressive setting, the most dramatic stage grouping,
the most artistic stage composition in static or fluent
forms.

" One feels as a critic that this principle of pictorial
emphasis should be applied in the photoplay." Yet it is
difficult to find many examples among the big photoplays that have hitherto been produced.   In *Carmen,*
for example, the climax begins when Don Jose starts
for Seville and ends when he slays Carmen and himself just outside the entrance to the arena.   But pictorially these tableaux are less interesting than the bull
fight, less stirring than the fight among the women in
the cigarette factory, and less beautiful than the marine
view at the opening of the play, three points in the
drama which have no very great plot value.   In *Joan,
the Woman* the climax begins when Joan is condemned
as a witch and ends when she is burned at the stake,
but the most impressive tableaux in the play are the
battle scenes of the armoured knights led by the inspired Joan of Arc.   *The Birth of a Nation,* wonderful as it is, cannot be looked upon as having any definite plot structure, which is undoubtedly a shortcoming

of the play.   It is really only a series of little dramas relating to a single period in American history.   But if we take the play as a whole we can perhaps agree that the most impressive picture as a picture, the tableau which we remember longest, is the gathering of the Ku Klux Klan.   Yet that gathering and the start of the ride is neither the beginning nor the end of a dramatic climax.   However, in *Intolerance* Griffith has managed to combine the most memorable pictures with the most significant action in the Babylonian story, the climax beginning when several thousand men assault the walls of the city, and ending when the massive gates, swung open by treachery, admit the enemy. The climax of the story of American contemporary life presented in *Intolerance* begins when The Boy ascends the scaffold, is most intense at the moment when the four executioners raise their knives to sever the cords which are to trip the scaffold, and ends when the pardon arrives by automobile.   Pictorially the end of the climax seemed cheap, because by 1916, when *Intolerance* appeared, the arrival of the racing automobile in the nick of time had become an outworn melodramatic device.   But the picture of the four men with their knives suspended above the white cords leading to the scaffold, ready to sever them at any moment, was a visual effect that made the spectator gasp, and that will be remembered by him as long as he remembers any part of *Intolerance*.   We do not say that a pictorial progression toward the climax of a photoplay can always be obtained, but we do say that when such progression of pictorial values can be obtained it will materially strengthen the play as a whole.

Another means of securing emphasis in a pictorial

progression is the acceleration of the tempo, as we have shown in the chapter on pictorial composition in fluent forms. The best example of this effect is shown in that part of *Intolerance* where the several stories are running parallel and approaching a climactic point. "The exposures become shorter and shorter, and our attention is flashed faster and faster from one story to the other, until the staccato style gives us the feeling of racing towards a dramatic goal."

An audience enjoys the progressive heightening of attention, which can be achieved in the four ways we have just indicated. But no audience in the world could endure such heightening attention for as much as an hour at a time, if the heightening were a mathematically perfect graduation, rising from second to second, and from minute to minute. Such a rise would strain the audience to the point of complete exhaustion. If attention is to rise to any height it is necessary, therefore, that it be allowed to rise in a rhythmical line. It is one of the laws of all human activity that periods of intense concentration must be relatively short, and are possible only after periods of comparative mental repose.

Let us symbolize the progression of dramatic attention by a loosely hung cable which ascends a hillside rhythmically over a row of posts. The angles, or apexes, of the cable would each represent a crisis, except the highest, which would represent the climactic point of the plot. The most dramatic pictures would, of course, coincide with these apexes of the cable. Those pictures which narrate incidents or situations would be on the up curves, since they create suspense. Still lower down on each curve would be the descriptive pictures, pictures which describe environment and character, and thereby lead to the succeeding rise of plot interest. And decorative pictures, pictures with no story interest at all, would be on the lowest points of each curve, or might even come on the down curve immediately after a crisis.

At present a common vice of photoplay production is the padding out of the plot with pictures that are merely descriptive or decorative, cutting them into the film in the most haphazard fashion. This vice can be turned into a virtue if the pictures which seem to be not really necessary to the plot proper are interpolated in such a way that they serve as rests for the spectator's attention at the time when such rests are needed. In any case rhythmical progression is an artistic merit which in no way needs defeat the unity or balance of a plot, but can be made an actual help in the distribution of dramatic emphasis in that plot.

The third main section of a plot is the solution. It begins at the point when the main conflict, having reached its highest intensity, takes an unmistakable turn in favor of one of the factors, or for some other reason reaches a definite end. Here again we may apply the principles of unity, balance, emphasis, and rhythm. The law of unity demands that the solution be an organic element of the play, that it come out of the play itself and not from the outside. Thus in *The Merchant of Venice* the solution comes out of the plot itself. It consists of the flaw in the bond, which was, of course, present in the bond at the time when it was first drawn up, although the audience was not aware of the fact. The solution comes as a surprise but not as a shock, because the audience realizes immediately that it is organically united with the complication. But suppose that the plot had been resolved, not by finding a flaw in the bond, but by having Shylock struck by lightning at the moment when he has received permission of the court to carry out the provision of the bond. That would violate unity by bringing a foreign element into the plot, because neither Jupiter, nor avenging Fate, nor the law of electricity have anything to do with this play.

Sometimes the solution may be foreshadowed in the premise of the play. In *The Second Mrs. Tanqueray* the climax is Mrs. Tanqueray's discovery that one of her former lovers has become engaged to marry her step-daughter, Ellean. Ellean is willing to forgive her fiancé, but cannot forgive her step-mother. Mrs. Tanqueray, who now sees no hope for the future, no possibility of redeeming her past, kills herself. This tragic end recalls what she had said at the beginning of the play: "Do you know, I feel certain I should make away with myself if anything serious happened to me." Another kind of organic solution is to be found in the type of play in which the end of the complication is the reverse of the beginning. Thus in *Twelfth Night* the main complication is due to the disguise which Viola assumed at the beginning of the play. The solution comes naturally when the characters concerned discover that Viola is in disguise.

Besides being an organic part of the play the solution should balance with the complication; that is, it should be sufficient for the complication. In *The Second Mrs. Tanqueray* the husband suggests, after the tragic discovery concerning his wife's former relation with Ellean's sweetheart, that they " get out of this place and go abroad again, and begin afresh." Had the play ended with that solution the audience would not have been satisfied. Every one would have felt that it was merely temporizing, merely a deceptive pause in a tragedy which would grow no less tragic as time went on. If the solution of a complication is a slight matter, easily arranged, we are given the alternative that the complication was not as serious as it seemed, that we as spectators have been tricked by the playwright. If the two families who are at feud in *Romeo and Juliet* patched up their quarrel for the sake of the lovers with a " Bless you, children! If you feel that way about it, go ahead and get married," we in the audience should feel that the feud was not a very sincere one after all, and that the joke was on those who had shed their blood in it. However the matter is viewed we see that a play cannot be convincing unless there is proper balance between solution and complication.

Such balance involves emphasis of ending. It means that a dramatic action terminates, instead of pausing before another period of progression. It means that if there is a sequel, that is an entirely different story, and may better be told some other day. The main suspense in the form of a definite question in the spectator's mind has now been relieved by a definite answer. He did not ask it in vain. His attention has marched up hill through the length of a play, but it has arrived somewhere, and the spectator has reached a higher level of experience. He has for an hour or so escaped from himself, has been diverted from the prosaic commonplaces of his own life; and the diversion has been edifying as well as entertaining.

Yes, Hamlet does get his revenge, but, he like the rest of us, gets revenge at too high a cost. No, Romeo and Juliet can never in life be happily united, but their sacrifice is the purchase of peace among those who survive. No, Lady Windermere did not insult Mrs. Erlynne, nor did she ever discover that the notorious woman was her mother, because even the Mrs. Erlynnes of the world are refined by fire, and will let no harm come to their own offspring. And so on, in all the masterpieces of drama, the action, after a vigorous march, halts permanently at the goal of some truth. This is the final downward curve in the rhythm of the play, and it leaves the spectator in a state of emotional repose. "The dramatic stir subsides, the picture on the screen fades out, and the satisfied spectator returns to himself."

But is he satisfied because he has just witnessed a play which was constructed according to the principles of unity, balance, emphasis, and rhythm? By no means do we make such a claim. We do not claim that the skeleton constitutes the life of the body, or that grammar constitutes the message of a sentence. But we do insist that, as the message cannot be expressed without proper grammatical construction, and as the heart cannot throb except within an organized frame, so drama cannot live, cannot have a permanently vital significance to the spectator, if it is fragmentary, unbalanced, uncentralized, unadapted to the rhythm of the spectator's mind and heart, if, in short, it is not breathed into a well organized form.

CHAPTER XIV

COMMERCIAL NEEDS

It has been pleasant to play the rôle of theorist and philosopher, to stand aloof and aloft and point out the faintly trodden or untravelled avenues which lead into the vistas of the ideal photoplay. But it must never be forgotten that between the starting point of our high purpose and the goal of accomplishment stands a practical man, the producer. He devotes his best thought and energy to the problem of making money for himself and his associates. His ideals are hardened into objects, and his objects drop back into commercial needs. These commercial needs no cinema composer can afford to ignore. As an artist he cannot express himself except through this interpreter, the business man. His photoplay, no matter how ideally conceived, is not born as art until it is exhibited. It must appear on the screen before thousands of people. It not only must be seen to be appreciated but it cannot be appreciated at all in any other way. And no photoplaywright, at least no beginner in the art, can exhibit his composition without the help of the manufacturer. In other arts it is not difficult to reach a public, even without a business man's faith in the product. A novelist, if he can find no other way, can publish a thousand copies of his book at a personal expense of about $500.00. An unappreciated poet can creep into print in his college literary magazine or in some village weekly. A playwright may direct an amateur production of his play at the casino of a summer resort. A pianist may play his own composition at the musicale of an indulgent host. A painter may exhibit his unsold painting at a tea in his own studio. But the photoplaywright must make his cinema composition a commercial commodity before it can exist as art. The producer may say, " I'll make money at any loss to art "; but the cinema composer may not say, " I'll produce art at any loss of money."

It behooves us therefore to study the needs of our indispensable ally, the manufacturer. His commercial aim is accomplished only when the box office test shows immediate results at low cost. The results must be immediate; the response from the exhibitors must be prompt. The film manufacturer does not speculate on the return from the next generation. He does not believe in paying storage charges on art, and he has not time to plant trees for his grandchildren. He buys, borrows, or steals the plots of yesterday, manufactures films today, rents them to the exhibitor tomorrow, and " scraps " them the day after tomorrow. All this briskness of business can be accomplished only by quick distribution following a vigorous campaign of advertising.

The producer insists that the photoplay he manufactures into a film must have advertising value. The play must have in itself something which can be sensationally presented in the newspapers or on bill posters, and may become the topic of conversation everywhere, in the club and the kitchen, on the way to school or baseball game, on the way to Wall Street or church. In short the play must have a " talking point." Some feature must be so strong that no one can possibly ignore it. Thus in a few recently released plays the " talking points " have been respectively as follows: the production cost a million dollars; a real ocean liner is sunk; a real horse plunges over a high cliff, actually killing himself and seriously wounding his rider; the heroine in leaping from the cliff into the sea broke the world's record for high diving; the " star " wears fifty different gowns during the play; a famous artist's model is shown in the nude; the bullfight is genuine; owing to the daring treatment of the sex theme children are not admitted. This list of " punches " can be extended indefinitely by any one who is not blind or deaf. Whatever objections we may make to these points we must admit that the advertisements which contain them will not go unread, and that the plays so exploited will not flicker across the screen unobserved.

Sometimes the astute manufacturer hitches his advertising " float " on to some bandwagon ahead by adopting a story already widely discussed, with a title all ready to be conjured with. He films a story of notorious vogue, *Three Weeks* or *Damaged Goods*. It may be undramatic; it may lack pictorial value; it may offer no opportunity for good acting; but it is saleable because the title is a good " talking point." At other times it is the performer who is familiar to the public. A prize fighter, or master of society dancing, or European adventuress, or slack wire contortionist is starred in some bit of studio hack work which, vapid as it is, pays for itself because of the reputation of a person, whose name is a good " talking point."

At the sound of all this talk the true artist heaves a sigh of distress, because he knows that in a perfect composition all the elements are so harmoniously blended, all the parts so perfectly correlated, that no one part is conspicuous or salient enough to be seized upon as a " talking point." He cannot find any " talking points " in the " Venus of Milo," or the " Sistine Madonna," or the Cathedral at Cologne, or *Macbeth*, or *Tannhäuser*, or *Crossing the Bar*. To him, only the composition as such is to be talked of. To him the masterpiece is classic because the artist has so carefully co-ordinated and subordinated all of his materials that a new perfection, a new totality has resulted. This philosophy of the true artist is sound; yet he must stop his sighing and learn to trim his sheets to the wind. If the publicity man must have his " feature," why then he must have it. But, while the publicity man is consulting his book of synonyms for superlatives, let the photoplaywright build his play around and up to the very level of the " feature." If the play is to contain a champion diver, let the plot turn on the height of the dive. If the play is to contain an artist's model of unusual physical beauty posing in the nude, let the whole tone, nature, and plot of the play be in perfect keeping, and the nude will seem no more extraordinary on the screen than in painting or sculpture.

The cinema composer who wants to give the " talking point " a genuine rôle as an organic part in the drama should observe the method of Shakespeare, whose dramas survive as art for all times despite their " talking points " for the day. Like the photoplay producers of today, he revamped popular old plays and adapted famous old stories. But he invariably bettered what he borrowed, and that vast difference between the borrowed and the bettered is Shakespeare. He gave the public some of the things they wanted, ghosts, fairies, witches, songs, combats and battles, alarums and excursions. But all of these Sixteenth Century " talking points " now seem entirely in the poetic key. He even gave the gaping groundlings (the prototypes of our " gallery gods ") acrobatic dances, wrestling matches, and low comedy episodes. And even these now seem an essential part of the pattern. Who would want to see Macbeth without the drunken porter scene? When the problem is met in this way the publicity man will have his advertisement and the artist his harmonious composition. And it is a safe wager that the spectator who came to be thrilled by a sensation will remain to be enthralled by pure art.

If, however, the photoplaywright finds it impossible to harmonize his whole composition with the " talking point " desired by the business man, he may still sail safely on the opposite tack. He may construct his photoplay so that the " talking point " becomes a mere excrescence which may be considered quite apart from the essential character of the play, so that the play will still be worth the price of admission in years to come when the " talking point " has gone stale or been forgotten.

Invariably the publicity man insists that the photoplay must be hitched to a " star." The play itself is looked upon as a necessary evil, and is indifferently alluded to as the " vehicle " of the " star," but above all, because of the advertising value, the " star " must shine. Now there can be no objection to composing a part for a performer providing an adequate play is built around the part. In fact, here the commercial need and the artists' ideal coincide. For a play must have emphasis somewhere, it must have a heart which gives vitality to the whole play, and that centre of life not only can, but should, be a human character. Sophocles, Shakespeare, Molière, Barrie, Shaw, all have focussed their attention on a single character in any particular play; and all of these masters have modelled their great characters more or less to suit the abilities of particular actors or actresses. But none of these men have made the mistake of looking upon a part as greater than the whole, nor upon a performer as greater than the character, and the result is that the author's creation lives on long after the interpreter has been forgotten. By all means let the photoplaywright keep his eyes on the " stars " of the motion picture studio, but let him remember also that they are merely the interpreters of the characters which he creates.

Most of all the advertiser is looking for novelty. And in this, as we have shown in the chapter on the psychology of the audience, he undoubtedly reflects popular taste. We are all straining our energies, spending our fortunes, travelling the world over, in our eagerness to see something new. But if this new thing is vital to us only because of its novelty, its life is only ephemeral, it must perish with the discovery. For novelty, by definition, cannot be permanent. A thing which is novel in 1910 is out of date in 1918. But if that thing possesses beauty, the beauty need not fade with the novelty. Italian opera, for example, was once a great novelty in England but its charm was more essential than the novelty, and that charm has developed into an inspiring beauty known throughout the civilized world. So in the photoplay there is no reason why novelty and dramatic truth and beauty should not exist concurrently. Of all the plot patterns in stage drama none is older than the "triangle" plot, the drama of husband, wife, and lover. Yet Bernard Shaw, once when fog-bound in Scotland for four days, composed an entirely new treatment of this ancient theme. His one act play *How He Lied to Her Husband* tells the story of a young poet who had written a volume of poems to a married woman, Aurora, and was surprised by the husband at the moment when he was about to elope with her. The poet when accused begins to lie, declaring that the poems were addressed to the dawn and not to the woman, and that he had, of course, never thought of her as a mistress. At this the husband is furious; he names a list of famous men who have tried to run off with his wife, and desires to know how the young man can have the impudence to insinuate that Aurora is not to be looked upon with the eyes of love. The whole affair ends amicably only when the poet confesses the truth. In this play an old initial situation is developed with novelty, because the dramatist has reached down beneath the hypocrisies of husbands, and brought into the blazing light of satire an interesting truth of human nature.

"The new twist" is what the motion picture advertiser calls such a variation as Shaw gave to the old "triangle" situation. "New twists" are not objectionable so long as they are natural twists and not contortions. Originality of plot is largely a matter of revealing old faces in new places. Human nature does not change with the history of the race. Natural love feels the same and manifests itself in the same way now as it did thousands of years ago; yet Hardy's *Return of the Native* is a different story from that of Anthony and Cleopatra. Hate is aroused in the same way now as in the days before primitive men had discovered fire or had perfected the crudest weapon; yet *The Siege of Troy* is a different story from the Battle of Verdun. The general traits in the normal human being are eternal verities. The individual may change, slightly through education, experience, suffering, or fortune; but his weaknesses are still there, only suppressed, and his virtues are the same, only cultivated. Humanity develops neither new sins nor new virtues. If an author could discover or invent a new sin, he would in one season become richer than Rockefeller. Even the production of a new virtue would create a mild sensation and would net him a fortune. But the particular combination of persons, things, places, and actions may be new. The lance is old but the machine gun is new; Mt. Olympus is old but the Woolworth Tower is new. Sheep herding is old, but the manufacture of motion pictures is new. Hence originality in dramatic composition involves the revelation of the familiar in the new, the combination of the eternal verities with passing circumstances. It is in this organization and integration that the alchemy of the artist's imagination may exert its magic. A block of marble may be as old as the hills; what new thing it shall become, whether a watering trough, a door step, a cornerstone, the keystone of an arch, or a statue of Venus depends on what a man sees in it and with what skill he can embody his vision.

Novelty, a famous "star," "punch," "the new

twist," and anything else that has advertising value is commercially desirable, nay, necessary, says the producer. It is said to be further necessary that the commodity advertised be produced at low cost. One of the evils in commercialized motion pictures is the practice of saving money on settings. Only recently one of the best of the big photoplay companies issued the injunction, " Write your story so that it can be played in any setting." In other words the cinema composer was enjoined to disregard one of his greatest functions, that of dramatizing the setting of his story, a function which, as we know, has greater scope and force in the photoplay than in any other narrative or dramatic art. It would be no more mad to ask the composer to plan his story so that it could be expressed through any stage group or cinematic motion that happened to suit the convenience and purse of the producer.

Another of the producer's means of economizing is seen in the constantly published objection to " costume plays." One producer justified his objection in this way: " The regular movie crowd don't think that a costume play is real. If they see a couple of guys with lace at their knees doing a few fancy stunts with swords, they don't think it's a real scrap. But if they see a Hoboken bartender hit a street car conductor over the noddle with a beer bottle, they know damn well it's a real fight." According to this testimony it would seem that the age of chivalry is gone, not only from life but from art as well. Another incident may prove even more illuminating to the reader. A successful playwright once made a photoplay adaptation of *Rip Van Winkle* and offered it to a well-known producer.

The producer read the scenario and handed it back with the remark that it was very well written, but that they did not desire "costume plays." Then with rare generosity he added, "I can give you a tip on how to fix it up so that it will go through. Make Rip an American army officer of today who gets drunk and dreams that he is Rip Van Winkle, and then wakes up and reforms." The playwright meekly suggested that no expense would be cut down by this, because the characters of the dream would have to be in the costume of the period. Stupid playwright! Listen to a shrewd refutation. "Sure, they'd have to wear some kind of costume, but it don't have to be correct, because, you see, it's only a dream and the army officer wouldn't know what the correct costume was." The answer to the first producer is that there is no disputing his customers' tastes. If the motion picture enthusiast asketh for a stone give him not bread. But the fact is that there are at present actually more "costume plays" on the screen than plays of modern life. To the second producer there is no answer, unless it be that he might save a few dollars by putting his dreaming army officer in a dress suit instead of a U. S. Army uniform. But there is a hope that the new generation of producers are waxing in wisdom, that, while they see the genuine drama of our contemporaries in everyday clothes, they are not blind to the pictorial appeal of the strange garb of distant lands and other days, when the realities of life were no less stern than now.

Expediency, even accident, is another factor in the reduction of expenditures. One photoplay director in New York said, "Scenario writers don't seem to realize that we have to work with what comes to hand,

For example, we may be on our way to a 'location' driving at fifty miles an hour, and may suddenly pass a beautiful water fall that we had never before heard of. Now the story has no action that calls for a water fall, but we can't afford to miss that beautiful picture, so we pose our 'stars' with the water fall as a background, and when we get home the scenario editor makes up a title for that picture." Again the dramatic value of setting is entirely ignored. In the same manner the personality of the hero or heroine of the author's intention may be warped to suit the temperament and ability of the particular performer who happens to be available at the time when the play is to be produced. Hence if the demand of expediency is to be observed a commercially desirable scenario should read something like this: " Let somebody (depending on what members of your company are available) do something (depending upon the circumstances) somewhere (depending on the 'sets' you have on hand and the 'locations' you discover) for from one to ten reels (depending on your contract with the distributor). "

In fact the producers' frequent request for " synopses only " is final proof that the accident-made play is commercially preferable to the play lovingly created by the individual artist. Let us see just how far the " synopsis only " system removes the author from his audience. First, the author's general idea, stated in the synopsis, is altered in general by the scenario editor or by the managing director of the corporation; second, the original idea is further adapted by the continuity writers who prepare the studio scenario; third, this scenario is interpreted by the director of the performers; fourth, his general interpretation is varied by the actors; fifth, their histrionic intentions are turned awry by the laws of optics and the mechanical limitations of photography; sixth the developed films are asssembled according to the judgment of the cutter and joiner; seventh, the finished photoplay may be further interpreted according to the speed and focussing of the projecting machine. No wonder a cinema composer becomes discouraged when he contemplates these seven interventions between himself and his audience. These interventions are not necessary; they do not, of course occur in the work of a man like Griffith. His conception, composition, supervision, and revision of such a play as *The Birth of a Nation* if set down in words on paper would make several volumes the size of this book. Imagine the producers asking Griffith to submit a three hundred, or even a twelve hundred word synopsis of his photoplay! Imagine what we would say of the director of some philharmonic orchestra if he sent out an advertisement like this: " We are in the market for music suitable to our musicians, our instruments, and our auditorium. Composers are requested to observe that we want ideas only and not the complete scores. Describe clearly in 500–750 words the general idea, the movements, melodies, motifs, etc. and leave the details to be worked out by us. We find by experience that our expert staff score writers in the office can work up the ideas in proper musical form more satisfactorily than the free lance composer, who really will waste his valuable time if he bothers with the complicated technique of the musical score, with its horizontal and vertical lines, circles, dots, flags, Italian abbreviations, etc., etc. We buy nothing but original ideas, and pay from $15.00 to $85.00 per idea." There is nothing exaggerated about this analogy, because the scenario is to the photoplay on the screen what the score is to musical performance.

Immediate results at low cost by the box-office test is the commercial need. But is the box-office test the safe and final test of art? It is the test of immediate sales; and the count is made before the goods are delivered. The box-office man balances his sheet before the audience has left the theatre. That the balance will be on the right side is assured by the advertising, by the present system of distribution, which amounts to a guaranteed market, and by the indifference of a large portion of the public who are not hyper-critical concerning the entertainment they get for a dime or a quarter. And even if a photoplay did please a particular crowd it does not follow that it will win lasting favour with the public. A photoplay which sold well in 1915 but brings no financial return in 1918 or 1919 must surely be without vitality or truth or abiding beauty. The art need of the world is permanent results at any cost by the continual test of discriminating critical taste.

The problem then is to reconcile commercial needs with artistic ideals. The solution is simple; and it does not consist in quarrelling with the producer. The producer is a business man, and the business man's business is to be a business man. Nor does the solution consist in quarrelling with the cinema composers. They do not always err through ignorance; for they must eat, and sleep, and clothe their children

the same as you. The solution lies with you who bu
tickets for motion picture entertainment, and i
consists in your making the production of good ar
more profitable than bad art.

THE END

PRINTED IN THE UNITED STATES OF AMERICA

INDEX

THE following pages contain advertisements of a few of the Macmillan books on kindred subjects.

THE ART OF THE MOVING PICTURE

By VACHEL LINDSAY

Author of "The Congo and Other Poems," etc.

Cloth, 12mo, $1.25.

Mr. Lindsay's book is one of the first to be written in appreciation of the moving picture. His purpose is to show how to classify and judge the better films.

The main thesis of the book is that the moving picture is essentially graphic rather than dramatic; the tendency of the art of the moving picture is away from its ostensible dramatic interest, towards the mood of the art exhibition. Moving pictures are pictorial; painting, sculpture and architecture shown in motion. He describes the types of photo plays, discusses the likeness of the motion picture to the old Egyptian picture writing, summarizes the one hundred main points of difference between the legitimate drama and the film drama, indicates that the best censorship is a public sense of beauty and takes up the value of scientific films, news films, educational and political films. The volume closes with some sociological observations on the conquest of the motion picture, which he regards as a force as revolutionary as was the invention of printing.

THE MACMILLAN COMPANY

Publishers   64-66 Fifth Avenue   New York

Making the Movies

By ERNEST A. DENCH

Cloth, $1.25.

An informing little book is this, describing the way in which moving pictures are made. There are chapters on Putting On a Photo Play, Movie Stars Who Risk Their Lives for Realistic Films, How Railroad Photo Plays are Made, How Fire Films are Taken, Making Cartoons for the Movies, Taking Films Under the Sea, The Work in a Film Factory, Aviation and the Movies, The Production of the Trick Photo Plays, and many other equally interesting topics. Mr. Dench knows the moving picture business from the inside and has written most entertainingly on his subject.

THE MACMILLAN COMPANY

Publishers **64-66 Fifth Avenue** **New York**

How to See a Play

By RICHARD BURTON

$1.25

This book puts in the hands of playgoers a helpful discussion of what is involved in the intelligent enjoyment of the theatre. It shows concisely and authoritatively what a play is in its development on English soil, in its changing forms and in its interesting new claims to-day, emphasis being placed upon the present situation. In addition to a sketch of the drama as literature and cultural appeal, and in its relation to society, the treatment includes a discussion of the artistic and constructive aspects of the play.

Dr. Burton, the President of the Drama League of America, is an engaging critic. His book is one which should interest all theatre-goers, inasmuch as it indicates how to see a play in order that it may give the greatest pleasure and profit to the spectator. Dr. Burton writes with a keen understanding of the drama and with the zest of one whose enjoyment of the theatre has not been lessened by many years of close study and analysis of its output.

———

THE MACMILLAN COMPANY
Publishers   64–66 Fifth Avenue   New York

Aspects of Modern Drama

By FRANK WADLEIGH CHANDLER

PROFESSOR OF COMPARATIVE LITERATURE AND
DEAN OF THE COLLEGE OF LIBERAL ARTS
IN THE UNIVERSITY OF CINCINNATI.

AUTHOR OF "ROMANCES OF ROGUERY" AND
"THE LITERATURE OF ROGUERY."

$2.00

A study of the best plays of the leading dramatists of the past quarter century. In this discussion of a literary topic of the hour, certain themes, artistic kinds, and ideas are considered, rather than the work of individuals, man by man. Specifically, the book illustrates, through the works of those of different race, the dramatic treatment of such characters as the wayward woman and the priestly hero; of such motifs as the tyranny of love, the influence of heredity and environment, and the ideal of honor; of such situations as are commonly involved in plays presenting scenes from married life; of such a plot as the eternal triangle; of such social problems as those of sex, divorce, racial antagonisms, and the relations of the rich and the poor; and of such artistic varieties as the naturalistic, the romantic, the symbolic, and the poetic drama. In two chapters concerned with the Irish plays, a national movement is described; and in most of the others appears incidentally some indication of the national, as well as the personal, peculiarities of writers, Spanish, Italian, French, German, Scandinavian, Russian or English. Owing to the novelty of its plan and the wealth of its material, it should prove of value both to the college student and to the ordinary reader and playgoer. The text contains analysis of some two hundred and eighty representative plays.

———

THE MACMILLAN COMPANY
Publishers   64-66 Fifth Avenue   New York

Lightning Source UK Ltd.
Milton Keynes UK
UKHW011547220621
385967UK00002B/387